MACHINE LEARNING

Master Machine Learning Fundamentals for Beginners, Business Leaders and Aspiring Data Scientists

MG Martin

TABLE OF CONTENTS

MACHINE LEARNING

Master Machine Learning Fundamentals For Beginners

MACHINE LEARNING

Master Machine Learning for Business Leaders

MACHINE LEARNING

Master Machine Learning for Aspiring Data Scientists

MACHINE LEARNING

Master Machine Learning
Fundamentals For Beginners

MG Martin

Introduction

There are a lot of computers out there that will have machine learning already on them, and you can even program these computers in order to learn from the inputs that the user is going to give it. This allows for the computer to give the results, and sometimes, the right answers that are needed even when it is working with a problem that is more complex. The input for this learning process, which we are going to call the learning algorithm (we will take a look at a few of these a little later on to see how they work), will be known as data training as well.

You have probably used this kind of technology when you are using a search engine to look up something online. Machine learning is the best option for you to use to make sure that you are able to make these search engines work for you. The program for the search engine is going to use machine learning to help the user get the search results that they need. And if it is set up in the right way, it is going to learn a bit from the choices of the user, helping it to become more accurate over time.

This is just one of the examples of technology that relies on machine learning. You will find that in addition to working on a search engine, including Google, this technology works with some spam messages and some other applications. Unlike some of the traditional programs that you may have learned how to use in the past, machine learning is going to be able to make adjustments and changes based on the behavior of the user. This helps you to have more options and versatility about the programs that you create.

The possibilities are endless!

Chapter 1

The Basics of Machine Learning

Now that we have had some time to go over a few of the basics that come with machine learning, it is time to delve in a bit more and learn how this process works, and why it is so important when you are trying to work on programs that are able to do what you want. When you are working with this kind of programming, you get the benefit of teaching a computer, or even a specific program, how to work with the experiences it has had in the past so that it can perform the way that it should in the future.

A good idea of how to illustrate this in the field is the idea of filtering out spam email. There are a few different methods that a programmer is able to use. One of the best and the simplest versions that you are able to work with for your program is to teach the computer how it is able to categorize, memorize, and then identify all of the different emails that are found in your inbox that you have gone through and labeled as spam. If it is successful, it should, at least most of the time, be able to tell when an email is spam and keep it out of your inbox.

While this is a memorization method that is easy to program, there are still a few things that could fail. First, you are going to miss out on a bit of inductive reasoning in program, which is something that must be present for efficient learning. Since you are the programmer, you will find that it is much better to go through and program the computer so that it can learn how to discern the message types that come in and that are spam, rather than trying to get the program to memorize the information.

To make sure that this process of machine learning is easy as possible, your goal would be to program the computer in a way that it is able to scan through any email that comes through the spam folder or any that it has learned is spam over time. From this scan, the program is going to be able to recognize different words and phrases that seem to be common in a message that is spam. The program could then scan through any of the newer emails that you get and have a better chance at matching up which ones should go to your inbox and which ones are spams.

You may find that this method is going to be a bit harder to program and take a bit more time, but it is a much better method to work with. You do need to take the proper precautions ahead of time with it to ensure that when the program gets things wrong (and it will make mistakes on occasion), you are able to go through and fix it fast.

There are many times that a person would be able to take a look at an email and with a glance figure out if it is spam or not. The machine learning program is going to do a pretty good job with this, but it is not perfect. You want to make sure that you are teaching it the right way to look at the emails that you get. And, sometimes, it will send perfectly good emails to the spam folder. But the more practice it gets with this and the more it learns how to work with what is spam and what isn't, the better it is going to get at this whole process.

Are there any benefits that come with machine learning?

There are a lot of different programming options that you are able to work with when it comes to making a program or doing code. Machine learning is just one of the options that you can work with. With that said, you may be curious as to what are the benefits of working in machine learning rather than one of the other options.

At this point, you may be curious as to why machine learning is going to be so great, and why you would want to make sure this is the method that you will use. There are a lot of options that you can program and code when you are working with machine learning, but we are going to focus on two main ones that are sure to make your programming needs a bit better.

The first concept that we are going to look at is the fact that machine learning means that you are able to handle any kind of task that seems too complex for a programmer to place into the computer. The second one is the idea that you are able to use the things that you learn from machine learning in order to adaptively generate all of the different tasks that you need to do. With these two concepts in mind, let's take a look at some situations where you may want to work with machine learning, where other codes and programming tricks and techniques are just not going to cut it.

Complicated Tasks

The first category that we are going to look at when it comes to using machine learning is with some of the more complicated tasks. There are going to be a few tasks that you are able to work on with your programming skills that, no matter how hard you try, just seem to not mesh together with traditional coding skills. These tasks may not be able to provide a high level of clarity that traditional coding needs, or they have too much in terms of complexity that comes with them.

You will find that the first category of tasks that we are going to look at here is going to be any that a person or some kind of animal would be able to perform. For example, speech recognition, driving, and even image recognition would fit into this category. Humans are able to do this without even thinking, but they would be really hard to teach a program to work with, especially if you are trying to use some conventional coding techniques. But machine learning will be able to step in and make sure that this works out the way that you would like.

The next issue that you may run into when working with the idea of machine learning is that it is going to handle some tasks and concepts were a human could run into some trouble. This may include doing things like going through huge amounts of data or at least a complex type of data. There are many companies who collect data about their customers to use in the future. But if the company is big, that is a ton of data to work with.

While a person would be able to do this and maybe come up with a decent analysis, it would take forever. And by the time they got all of that data sorted through, there would probably be new data that needs some attention, and they would fall behind and be using outdated information. With machine learning, the business would be able to go through this information quickly and come up with some smart predictions that would be easy to use and promote the business forward.

You may find that you can use some of the concepts that come with machine learning to help with projects that work with genomic data, weather prediction, and search engines. There is going to be a lot of information that is seen as valuable with all of the different sets of data, but it is hard to find the time and the energy to go through this information. And it may not be done in a manner that is timely. But machine learning can step in and get it done.

If you have already spent some time learning about traditional programming and you know how to use a traditional coding language, then it is likely that you already know some of the cool things that you are able to do with them. But there are a lot of different things that will be more useful as technology progresses even more that machine learning will be able to help you do.

Adaptively Generated Tasks

You will find that conventional programs can do a lot of really cool things, but there are some limitations to watch out for. One of these limitations is that these conventional programs are a little bit rigid. Once you write out the code and implement it, the codes are going to stay the same all the time. These codes will do the same thing over and over unless the programmer changes the code, but they can't learn and adapt.

There will be times when you are working on a program that you want to act in a different manner or react to an input that it receives. Working with a conventional program will not allow this to happen. But working with machine learning allows you to work with a method that teaches the program how to change. Spam detection in your email showed a good example of how this can work.

Machine learning is easier to work with than you think.

Yes, there are going to be some algorithms and other tasks that come with machine learning that are more complex and take some time to learn. There are a lot of examples of what is possible with machine learning that is actually pretty simple. Your projects are going to be more complicated compared to what you saw with regular programming, but machine learning is able to take those complicated tasks and make them easier. You will be surprised at how easy it is to use the programming techniques of machine learning to do tasks like facial recognition and speech recognition.

Machine learning is often the choice to work with because it has the unique ability to learn as it goes along the process. For example, we are able to see how this works with speech recognition. Have you ever used your smartphone or another device to talk to it and had some trouble with it being able to understand you, especially in the beginning? Over time, though, the more that you were able to use the program, the better it got at being able to understand you. In the beginning, you may have had to repeat yourself over and over again, but in the end, you are able to use it any way that you would like and it will understand you. This is an example of how machine learning is able to learn your speech patterns and understand what you are saying over time.

While machine learning is going to be able to work with a lot of different actions that may be considered complex, you will find that it is really easy to work with some of the codes that go with it and you may be surprised at how a little coding can go a long way. If you have already worked with a bit of coding and programming in the past, then you will be able to catch on quick, and it won't take much longer for those who are brand new to the idea either.

What are some of the ways that I can apply machine learning?

Now that we know a bit more about the different benefits that come with machine learning, it is time to move on and learn a bit more about some of the other things that you are going to be able to do with this as well. As you start to work with the process of machine learning a bit more, you will find that there are a lot of different ways that you are able to use it and many programmers are taking it to the next level to create things that are unique and quite fun.

You may also start to notice that there are many different companies, from startups to more established firms that are working with machine learning because they love what it is able to do to help their business grow. There are so many options when it comes to working with machine learning, but some of the ones that you may use the most often are going to include:

Statistical research: machine learning is a big part of IT now. You will find that machine learning will help you to go through a lot of complexity when looking through large data patterns. Some of the options that will use statistical research include search engines, credit cards, and filtering spam messages.

Big data analysis: many companies need to be able to get through a lot of data in a short amount of time. They use this data to recognize how their customers spend money and even to make decisions and predictions about the future. This used to take a long time to have someone sit and look the data, but now machine learning can do the process faster and much more efficiently. Options like election campaigns, medical fields, and retail stores have used machine learning for this purpose.

Finances: some finance companies have also used machine learning. Stock trading online has seen a rise in the use of machine learning to help make efficient and safe decisions, and so much more!

As we have mentioned above, these are just three of the ways that you can apply the principles of machine learning in order to get the results that you want in order to aid in your business or even to help you create a brand new program that works the way that you want. As technology begins to progress you will find that new applications and ideas for how this should work are going to grow as well.

Are there certain programs I can use machine learning with?

By now, you shouldn't be too surprised that there are a lot of different programs that you are able to utilize with machine learning, and many more are likely to be developed as time goes on. This makes it a really fun thing to learn how to work with and your options are pretty much going to be limited only by your imagination and coding skills.

There are a lot of different applications where you are able to use machine learning, and you will find that each of them can show you a different way that machine learning is going to work. Some examples of what you are able to do when you start to bring out machine learning will include:

Search engines: A really good example of machine learning is with search engines. A search engine can learn from the results that you push when you do a search. The first few times, it may not be as accurate because there are so many options, and you may end up picking an option that is further down the page. But as you do more searches, the program will learn what your preferences are and it can get better at presenting you with the choices that you want.

Collaborative filtering: This is a challenge that a lot of online retailers can run into because they will use it to help them get more profits through sales. Think about when you are on a site like Amazon.com. After you do a few searches, you will then get recommendations for other products that you may want to try out. Amazon.com uses machine learning in order to figure out what items you would actually be interested in, in the hopes of helping you to make another purchase.

Automatic translation: If you are working with a program that needs to translate things, then you are working with machine learning. The program needs to be able to look at a document and then recognize and understand the words that are there along with the syntax, grammar, and context of the words that are there. And then, if there are mistakes in the original document, this can make it harder for the program to learn along the way. The process of machine learning needs to teach the program how to translate a language from one point to another, and if it is able to do this with more than two languages, then it needs to learn all the different rules of grammar between each one. The programs that are out right now for this are still in beginner stages, so it's important that machine learning is used to improve them.

Name recognition: Another option that you are able to use with machine learning is the idea of name identity recognition. This is when the program is set up so that it will recognize different entities including places, actions, and names when it is reading through a document. You will be able to work with a program and ask it to digest and then comprehend the information that it reads. This helps to find the information that is in the document much faster than you have to read through it all.

Speech recognition: We talked about this one a bit before. But you will find that speech recognition is a great example of how you are able to work with machine learning. Speech recognition can be difficult. There are so many speech patterns, differences between ages and genders, and even languages and dialects that it is hard to make any kind of program that will do well with recognizing the speech patterns of those who talk to it. But since machine learning can learn as it goes, you get the benefit of having it get more familiar with your way of talking. There are going to be some mistakes and issues along the way. But if you are able to work with it and get through those early stages, the program will be able to learn and you get the benefit of having a program that understands your requests.

Facial recognition: And the final thing that we are going to take a look at is the idea of facial recognition. This is where the program is able to look at the face of a person and recognize who they are. Or at least it will be able to tell if that person has security clearance to be in a certain area, for example. It is going to go through a series of learning processes in order to tell who is able to be on the system and who should be turned away in the process.

There are so many cool things that you are able to do when you start to bring in some machine learning. And while all of these sound hard and would be nearly impossible with the conventional forms of programming, you will find that they can be easy and a lot of fun to work with when you are doing machine learning. This book will take some time as we progress to show you some of the different types of machine learning and how you are able to use those to do some of the tasks above.

Chapter 2

Artificial Intelligence vs. Machine Learning

The next thing that we need to take a look at here is the idea of artificial intelligence, and then look to see if this and machine learning are the same thing. To start, data science, as we explored in the first chapter, is going to be a really broad term that includes a lot of concepts that all come together. Topics that come with data science are going to include data mining, big data, artificial intelligence, and machine learning to name a few. Data science is always growing since it is a newer field, and understanding how the different concepts come around and act will make a big difference.

Statistics is really important when it comes to data science, and it can also be used often when it comes to machine learning. You would be able to work with classical statistics, even at the higher levels, so that the data set is going to stay consistent throughout. But the way that you use it will depend on what kind of data you are using and how complex the information is.

It is important to understand the difference between the categories of artificial intelligence and machine learning. There are some instances where they can be very similar, but there are some major differences, which is why they are considered two different things. Let's take a look at each of these to ensure that we understand how they both work in data science.

What is Artificial Intelligence?

The first thing that we need to take a look at is the idea of artificial intelligence and see how it is different than machine learning. To someone who may not understand how these two concepts work, and who is not familiar with the whole process, it may seem that the two of these are going to be the same thing. But there are actually some key differences that are important when you are working with this process.

To start, artificial intelligence, or AI, is a term that was first seen in the world of computer science in the 1950s thanks to John McCarthy. This process is a method that you would use in many devices in the manufacturing world so that these devices are able to copy the human capabilities when it comes to various mental tasks.

In the past few years though, the term is a bit different than it was in the beginning. You will still find though, that while the term has changed a bit, the idea is still basically the same. When you work to implement this AI, you are going to enable the program or the machine that you are using, to operate and think in a manner that is similar to what we see in the human brain. This is a great benefit that means that when you see a device with AI, you are going to become efficient at completing tasks the same way that the human brain can.

For those who are not used to the world of technology, it seems like machine learning is going to be the same thing as AI, but there are some differences that can show up between these two. Keep in mind as we go through this book that machine learning is not going to be the same as AI, and that is a big critical component to making sure you get the results that you want with these learning algorithms.

Machine Learning

Now that we have taken a look at the idea that comes with AI, it is important to take a look at machine learning and how it is different.

First, you will find that machine learning is a newer concept and idea compared to AI and other forms of data science, even though it has been around for about 20 years so far. Even though it is newer than some of the other options, it is still one that has had its own impact when it comes to the world of technology.

When you take a look at machine learning, we are specifically focusing on a type of data science that is going to have your program learn from the input and the other data that a user gives to it. It can learn how to make predictions that can be used in the future.

For example, when you are looking to use a search engine, you may go through and type in the search query that you would like to work with. You will type it into the search bar and then click on enter. The search engine, which is going to be based on machine learning, is going to go through and look through all of the pages available online, which could be quite a few based on the topic, and then pull up what is available.

The goal of this is for the program to pull up the search results that are going to match what you want the most. But since each person is going to find different information pertinent and valuable, it is possible that for the first bit you use this, the information is not always going to be on top of the page. You may have to scroll down a bit to find the results that you need. The neat thing though is that the search engine, powered by machine learning, is going to see that you scrolled down, and will take notes.

Over time, as you use the search engine more and more, it is going to become better at guessing which results you will want to click on, based on the clicks that you did in the past. This is why it becomes the one that you want to use the most often. As you use it more and more, you may then find that you will be able to click on one of the top options to get the results that you want rather than having to scroll all the way down the page.

You can imagine that this is just one of the many, many examples that you are able to use when it comes to machine learning. In fact, there are so many times when you will be working on a program with your computer that is more complex and machine learning will be able to step in and do the work for you. Plus, it is going to be able to do it at a speed and efficiency that the human brain is not able to handle.

For example, data mining is really going to benefit when you are working with machine learning. With data mining, there is a lot of data, maybe millions of different points that you need to sort through. While it is possible for a person or two to go through that information and try to figure out what is there, this is going to take a lot of time and be really slow. The person may miss out on some information that is critical. And if it is for a business, new data points are going to come in faster than the individual is able to sort through.

But when you work with machine learning, all of that data can be sorted through quickly and efficiently. And then you can ask the program to bring back some results from all of that data, depending on the learning algorithm that you choose to use, in order to help them make some predictions on how they should react in the future based on that data.

There are just so many cool things that you will be able to do when you choose to work with machine learning and some of the different sections of data science. But each of them, even though they may seem to have a lot of similarities like AI and machine learning, are going to be a little bit different and can work on your programming in different ways. Understanding how this works and putting it all together can really help to make things easier to work with overall.

Additional Exploration

Both machine learning and artificial intelligence are big words in the world of technology and they are often going to be used by those in the industry interchangeably because they seem to be so similar. There are some big differences in them, like what we have talked about before, but the perception that they are similar can sometimes lead to a lot of confusion. Both terms are going to show up a lot when we are talking about technological changes, analytics, and even big data, and they have both been able to make big changes in the field together and on their own.

The best answer to this is that artificial intelligence is going to be a broad concept of machines being able to carry out a task in technology, and it can do this in a way that people see as "smart". But with machine learning, we are looking at the current application of AI that is based around the idea that we should really be able to just give the machines the access to the data that they need, and then we can let them take that data and learn on their own.

Once these kinds of innovations were put in place, it didn't take long before engineers were able to realize that they didn't have to spend a lot of time teaching a machine or a computer how to do all of the steps that it needed in each process. This is what was done in the past, and it took a lot of time and was not all that efficient overall.

Neural networks, which we will talk about in a bit more detail later, was a key point in helping to teach a computer or another system how to act and understand the world in the way that we do, while still keeping some of the biggest advantages over just having a person do the work including a lack of bias, accuracy, and speed.

This idea of neural networks is a computer system that has been designed to work by classifying information in the same way that the brain of a human does. If it is done in the right manner, with the right kinds of rewards and consequences for getting the answer right or wrong, then it is going to be able to recognize different things like images, and then classifying these images based on the elements that are found inside. This is one of the biggest ways that machine learning, which is a vehicle of AI in many cases, is able to really learn and do some of the amazing things that we come to expect.

Both artificial intelligence and machine learning are able to offer us a lot today. With a promise of making some mundane tasks more automated, and the ability to offer us a lot of creative insight, it is no surprise that industries from all sectors, including manufacturing, healthcare, and banking, are taking advantage of these technologies. These have been so successful that both machine learning and AI are now products that are being sold on a consistent basis.

In particular, the ideas that come with machine learning are really soaring and many marketers are working to show this to businesses of all kinds. Even though there is a lot that you can do with AI, machine learning is seen as the newer version in a lot of cases, which means that a lot more focus is being put on it compared to some of the other technologies that are out there, like AI.

The cool thing is that you are able to use both of these to help you get your data sorted out and to help with some of the other complex situations that you need to get done from one day to the next in your business. This book is going to focus mainly on how to work with machine learning, but you will find that AI has a very big place, even still, when it comes to working with the technological field.

Chapter 3

Unsupervised Machine Learning and Data Scrubbing

Now that we have had a chance to talk about the benefits and the types of supervised machine learning that you are able to work with, it is time to move on to the second type of machine learning that you are most likely to use in your work.

There are going to be many times when you will need to pull out some of the algorithms that are needed with supervised machine learning. And then there are going to be times when this kind of learning is not quite right for your needs, and it is time to bring out the algorithms that go with unsupervised machine learning.

As a review, remember that when you are working with the supervised machine learning, you are going to show the computer some examples of how it should behave, and then the computer is going to learn how you would like it to respond to different scenarios. There are a lot of different types of programs that are going to need to use this, and learning how to use it can make a big difference in the results that you get.

But you can already think of a few times when this is not going to work out that well for you. Maybe you are thinking about all of the thousands or more examples that you would have to show the computer in order to get this kind of method to work. Sure, you could take the time to do this, but it can take a lot of time and get really tedious in the process. Plus, there are some kinds of programs were just showing it examples are not going to work well, or it won't be that practical for the program that you need.

When you reach into some of these issues, it is likely that you need to look for a different type of algorithm, and this could be unsupervised machine learning. This is the next method of machine learning that you are going to look at. Unsupervised machine learning is going to be the type that you would use to allow the program to learn on its own, rather than showing it all of the examples and teaching it. If supervised learning is like learning in the classroom, then unsupervised learning is going to be independent learning.

The program is going to be able to learn on its own based on any information that the user is going to give to it when you use unsupervised machine learning. It is possible that it isn't going to give the best answer that you would like, and it is going to make mistakes on occasion. But if you set up this kind of algorithm in the proper manner, it is going to be able to learn from these mistakes. Basically, when you bring out the algorithms that you would use with this kind of learning, it basically means that the program is going to be able to figure out and analyze any of the data patterns that it sees and make good predictions on that information based on the input that the user decides to give to it.

Just like what we saw when we were working with supervised learning, there are a few options that the coder is able to use with algorithms. No matter which of the algorithms you need for the coding that you do, it is still possible for that algorithm to take the data and then do some restructuring of it so that the data falls into classes.

When this restricting is done, it is easier for the coder, or anyone else, is able to look through all of the data and determine what is there and what is the most important. You are going to enjoy working with this kind of machine learning because it is going to be set up so that the computer is going to be able to do the work of learning for you, rather than writing out all of the instructions and having to do the work to teach the computer on its own.

One example of how this kind of machine learning is when a company would like to read through a ton of data in order to make predictions about the information that it sees. It can also be a way that you can get your search engine to work while still providing you with results that are as accurate and valuable as possible.

When you are ready to work with unsupervised machine learning, you will get the benefit of working with a few different algorithms to help you get it all done. The most common algorithms that you need to learn any time you want to work with this kind of learning includes:

Clustering algorithms

Neural networks

Markov algorithm

What is Reinforcement Learning?

When you are looking at reinforcement machine learning you may notice that it is going to be a bit different compared to some of the others. It shows a bit of similarity compared to unsupervised machine learning, but the algorithms are a bit different, and we are working with the idea of trial and error rather than teaching the machine.

Whenever you want to work with reinforcement machine learning, you are doing a method that is more of a trial and error. This method can be similar to working with a smaller child. When the child does something that you do not approve of, you will tell them that they did it wrong or you will ask them to stop. If they do an action that you approve of, you can do another action to tell them that you approve, such as praising them or giving them positive reinforcement. Over time the child is going to learn what you see as acceptable behavior or not. With the right type of reinforcement each time, the child will strive to do what you want. This is similar to how the reinforcement machine learning works. The program will learn, based on trial and error, how you want it to behave in each situation.

Reinforcement machine learning works on the idea of trial and error and requires that the application use an algorithm that helps it to make decisions. It is a good one to go with any time that you are working with an algorithm that should make these decisions without any mistakes and with a good outcome. Of course, it is going to take some time for your program to learn what it should do. But you can add this into the specific code that you are writing so that your computer program learns how you want it to behave.

Data Scrubbing and Preparation

Before you build a machine learning model, you should collect the data and prepare it to ensure that it can be used to train the machine. This is not enjoyable work, but it is essential that you do this so your model is accurate. Engineers often spend hours writing code before they realize that there is something amiss with the data. It is for this reason that experts mention that it is important to clean and scrub the data before it is used to train a model.

Many companies have teams dedicated to cleaning the data, but there are many companies that do not worry about this. It is for this reason that most analyses performed using unclean data does not provide accurate results. The goal of any engineer should first be to clean the data, or at least try to clean it to the best of their ability.

Quickly Check Your Data

When you obtain any data set, new or old, you should always verify the contents in that data set using the .head() method.

```
import pandas as pd

df = pd.read_csv('path_to_data')

df.head(10)

>>
```

You will receive some output when you run the above code. This will help you ensure that the data has been picked up from the correct file. You should now look at the types and names of the different columns in the data set. More often than not you will receive data that is not exactly what you are looking for like dates, strings, and other incomprehensible information. Therefore, it is important that you look for these oddities in the beginning.

You should now look for the index that is associated with the data frame. You can do this by calling on the function called '.index.' You will receive the following error if there is no index attached to the data frame: AttributeError: 'function' object has no attribute 'index.' You can use the following:

```
#Check the index values

df.index.values

#Check if a certain index exists

'foo' in df.index.values

#If index does not exist

df.set_index('column_name_to_use', inplace=True)
```

You have now checked most of the data and are aware of the data types. You will also know if there are any duplicates in the columns in the data set and whether an index has been assigned to the data frame. The next step is to identify the columns that you want to include in your analysis and the columns that you want to get rid of.

What to Do With NaN

If you want to identify a way to fill in the blank data or remove any errors in the data set, you should use the two methods dropna() and fillna(). The process of filling blank data and getting rid of errors becomes faster when you use these two methods. That being said, you must ensure that you document every step that you perform so another user can easily understand what it is that you are trying to achieve.

You can fill the NaN values with the mean or median value of all the numbers or with strings depending on the data type. Many engineers are still unsure of what they can do with malformed or missing data because they must decide what to do with the data set depending on the type of analysis that he or she is performing.

Experts suggest that engineers use their best judgment or speak to the people they are working with to decide on whether they should remove blank data or fill it using a default value.

Chapter 4

Top Applications

We have spent quite a bit of time learning about all machine learning is, and how amazing it can be for some of the programming that you want to be able to work with. There are so many different things and applications that are going to use this type of coding, and as technology starts to become more advanced and changes in the future, it is likely that more and more applications are going to be developed at the same time as well.

There are already a lot of applications that are going to be used on a regular basis, along with machine learning. Some of the most common ones include options like image recognition, speech recognition, and predictions for many major companies trying to sort through their data and know which way they should take their business in the future. With that in mind, let's explore a bit more about some of the top applications that you will be able to use with machine learning.

Image Recognition

One of the most common applications of machine learning is image recognition. Most phones and many laptops are going to be able to use this kind of algorithm to help them recognize the faces of the users who are on them. There are a lot of different situations where you may want the technology that you have to be able to classify a certain object and tell you what is in the image. The measurements of each digital image that you want to pull up are going to give the user an idea of the output of each pixel in the image.

So, let's say that you want to look at an image that is all in black and white, the intensity that comes with all of the pixels that are in that image would help because they serve as the measurement. If the image ends up having M*M pixels, then we would denote this as having a measurement of M^2.

The cool thing is that when the machine has this kind of software put on it, it can go into the picture and split up the pixels so that you end up having three different measurements. These help you to know what the intensity level of the three primary colors, namely RBG, are. So, with the idea of M*M from before, then there are going to be three M^2 measurements.

Face detection is one of the most common categories that comes with image recognition software, and it is used in order to help detect whether the image has a face or not. There can also be a different category that is added in that allows you to make a new category for each person in your database.

You can also work with a part that is known as character recognition. When you add this to your machine learning program, you are able to segment out each piece of writing into the images of small sizes where each image contain one character. These categories are going to be comprised of the 26 letters of the English alphabet, as well as the first ten numbers and any special characters that come with it.

As you can see, there are already a lot of cool things that you are able to do when it comes to image recognition. It can even help you to do security checks and recognition on some social media sites. Being able to recognize what is inside an image and developing more and more technology to help with this is definitely something that we should expect in the future.

Speech Recognition

Speech recognition is when an application is able to take spoken words, and either translates it back into some actual text or when it is able to follow a command of what you are telling it to do, including what we see with Amazon Echo and other similar products. Experts are going to refer to this kind of application in a few different ways, including Computer Speech Recognition, Speech to Text, and Automatic Speech Recognition.

The programmer is able to use this in order to take spoken words and then trains the machine in order to recognize speech and to convert the words into text. Google and Facebook are two mainstream programs that using this kind of method to help train their machines. The machines use measurements in order to represent the signal of speech. These signals are then further split up into distinct phenomes and words. The algorithm, if it is set up the right way, uses different kinds of energies in order to represent the signals that the speech sends out.

The details that you are able to see with this representation are going to be a bit more than what we will talk about in this book, but it is important to know that all of the signals are going to relate back to real signals. Applications that are out there that help with speech recognition will also be able to include an interface for the voice user, some of these including things like voice dialing and call routing on your phone. Depending on the application, these are able to use data entry and some of the other simple methods that are used to process information.

Predictions

Let's take some time to use our imagination here in order to think about how a bank works. In this scenario, a bank is going to try and calculate the probability of whether an applicant for a loan is going actually to pay for their loans or default on repayment. To help them to calculate this kind of probability of risk, the system must first to be able to identify, clean, and classify the data that is available in groups.

The analysts are going to classify the data based on certain criteria. Prediction is one of the most sought after uses of machine learning. And there are so many ways that it can be utilized. First, you will find many companies want to be able to use this in a way to help them to figure out whether or not they should take one action or another in order to help them to grow. This can help a bank figure out if one of their applicants is going to keep paying the loan. It can help retailers to figure out the best way to advertise their products to their customers, and it can help to figure out how sales will do in the future.

Anyone who has to do forecasts and make guesses about the way that their business should go in the future will benefit from this kind of technology. Instead of having to sift through all of the information on their own and hoping they get it right, or being new to the business and not having enough experience to back up the decisions, these business owners and decision makers are able to go in and use some of the algorithms of machine learning.

Machine learning, including a few of the algorithms that we talked about in this book, are going to be able to take a look at all of the information and data. This could include information on customers, their buying habits, inventory, and past sales to name a few. It will then compute the information, and show the likely outcome, based on past events, that something is going to work for you or not. This makes it easier to know which decisions need to be made for your business.

Of course, these are not going to be accurate all of the time. There are going to be times when the predictions are going to be wrong, such as if there is a big change in the industry or the economy ends up going down. But they are going to be more accurate than what most humans can do on their own. And having someone who watches the market and prepares in case something drastic does change, and doing these predictions on a regular basis will make a big difference.

Medical Diagnosis

Machine learning is going to provide us with a number of methods, tools, and techniques that a doctor is able to use in their field to solve diagnostic and prognostic problems. Doctors and patients can both use these techniques in order to enhance their medical knowledge and analyze the symptoms in order to figure out what the prognosis.

The results that you are able to get from this kind of analysis can be very valuable. You will find that it is able to really open up the medical knowledge that most doctors have. Even skilled professionals are going to find there are certain conditions and treatments that they don't know about, and being able to work with machine learning can help them to do their job more efficiently. Doctors are able to use this machine learning in order to identify the irregularities in unstructured data, the interpretation of continuous data and to monitor results efficiently.

The use of this and how successful it is will help it to integrate computer-based systems with the healthcare environment and will greatly increase opportunities to enhance and even improve the types of treatments provided.

When we are looking at a medical diagnosis, the interest that comes with this is to establish the existence of the disease, and then the doctor needs to identify the disease accurately. There are different categories for each disease that are under consideration, and then they can add in a category for different diseases that may not be present. Then, with the help of machine learning, it helps to improve the accuracy of a diagnosis and analyzes the data of the patients. The measurements used are the results of the many medical tests conducted on the patient. Doctors can identify the disease using these measurements.

Statistical Arbitrage

The next thing that you are going to be able to use machine learning is known as statistical arbitrage. This is a term used in finance, so if you are working in this kind of field, it is going to be a good one to focus on. This refers to the science of using trading strategies to help identify some of the securities that are short term in which one can invest.

When using these kinds of strategies, the user is able to implement in an algorithm on an array of securities based on the general economic variables and the historical correlation of the data. The type of measurement that you are going to be able to use will help to resolve any problems that you have with estimation and classification. The assumption is that the stock price is going to always stay near its historical average overall.

Another strategy to focus on is the **index arbitrage**. This is strategy that relies on the methods we have discussed with machine learning. The linear regression, as well as the support vector regression algorithms that we talked about before, are going to be so useful in helping the user calculate out the different prices that you will see with the funds and the stocks that you are interested in. and if you add in the principal component analysis, you will see that the algorithm breaks the data into various dimensions, which are used to identify the trading signals as a mean reverting process.

When it comes to investing there are a lot of different parts that come into play and being able to keep them organized along knowing how to use them with machine learning can take some practice. The buy, hold, sold, put, call or do nothing are just a few of the categories under which the algorithm places these securities under, based on what you want to do with it overall. The algorithm is then going to get to work helping you to calculate out the returns that you should expect in the future on each security. These estimates are going to help the user decide which security they want to buy and which security they would like to sell.

Learning Associations

The final application that we are going to focus on when it comes to machine learning is known as the learning association. This is basically the process of trying to develop a good insight into the association between different groups of products that you have. There will be several products that are responsible for revealing this association, even if the two products or variables seem like they are completely unrelated. This kind of algorithm is useful because it takes into account the buying habits of the customers in order to figure out the best associations that are present.

One of these types of learning associations that can be used is known as basket learning analysis. This one, in particular, is going to deal with studying the association between products that were purchased by different customers. It is a type of application that works well at showing us how machine learning works.

With this one, we will assume that our Customer A bought product X. Based on this purchase, we are going to use the options from machine learning in order to identify whether she is going to purchase product Y based on how these two products are associated together.

If you have a new product that comes into the market, the association that was there between the previously existing products will also change. Sometimes it will change quite a bit, and sometimes the products are not related much to the new one, and their association is not going to change all that much. If one already knows the relationships between various products, they are able to go through and identify the right product to recommend to their customers.

And this is also one of the reasons that a lot of companies are happy to introduce their products in pairs, rather than individually. This helps them to promote two products, and make a bigger sale by predicting the needs that their customer will have ahead of time and then meeting the need. If the customer sees two related products that go together and they are released at the same time, they are more likely to purchase both of these products together, knowing that they go together, and it increases the purchasing power and the capital for the company.

Big Data analysts work with machine learning on a regular basis in order to help them figure out what relationship is there when it comes to different products from the same company. The algorithms can often use the idea of probability and statistics, like we talked about earlier, to help come up with the relationship that is present in these products, and to help the company figure out which other products the customer is likely to purchase after they purchase the first one.

As you can see here, there are a number of different ways that machine learning is able to be used. And it can be used across a wide variety of different industries and in many ways. Whether it comes to using it to recommend products for a customer, you use it to make some predictions, or for some other reason, you will find that the things that machine learning is able to do already, and the applications that it is likely to be able to do in the future are already pretty amazing.

Chapter 5

Additional Algorithms

In this book, we have already talked about quite a few of the algorithms that you are able to use when it comes to working with machine learning. There are a lot of different ones that are available to make life a bit easier as well, but now, we are going to cover a few more of the ones that you may find useful if you are trying to grow your skills. Some of the other machine learning algorithms that you are able to use in order to help train any machine that you are using includes:

Dimension Reduction Methods

When we take a look at some of the databases that you may be using, it is possible that there could be millions or more records and variables. And you will need to use all of these variables in order to derive a good training data set. It is impossible to conclude that the variables are not going to be dependent on one another with any kind of correlation between them. It is important for you to remember that there are often going to be more than one similarity between the variables. In this kind of situation, the predictor variable is going to be correlated in some way, and this is often going to have some kind of effect on the output.

Now, there are going to be times when there is a lot of instability arises in the solution set when there is multicollinearity between the variables leading to incoherent results. For example, with this, if you are trying to look at more than one regression, there are multiple correlations between the predictor variables that have a significant impact on the output set.

However, individual predictor variables may not have a significant impact on the solution set. But, you may find that even when the programmer is able to identify a way to remove this kind of instability (and they will often strive to make that happen), then there are still going to be times when their user, or the one who is going to use the program at some point, may include variables with a high level of correlation between them. When this does happen, the algorithm will need to focus more on some parts of the input vector more than to the others.

Now, you may have a data set that ends up with more than one kind of predictor variable, and when this happens, there is going to be a new complication that shows up. This complication is going to be where the algorithm must identify a model between the predictor and the variables that end up responding. This situation is going to complicate the analysis and its interpretation and violates the principle of parsimony.

So, what is this principle all about? This principle is going to state that as an analyst who is using machine learning, should always stick to a certain number of predictor variables, which makes it easy for human beings, as well as machines, in order to interpret the results. It is tempting to go through and retain a lot of different variables. But when this happens, there is going to be some possibility of a problem known as overfitting. You can try to do this, but it is likely that it is going to hinder the analysis that you are able to get in the long run. Picking out one predictor to work with and getting everything else to fit with it is going to be the best.

The goal of working with this kind of method in machine learning is that we want to use the structure of correlation among the different variables of prediction. The reason that this is going to be done in this method is to help the programmer work towards the following goals:

- Reduce the number of components for prediction in the set of data that you are using.

- It can ensure that the components that you are using for predictions are going to continue to be independent of one another.

- It can predict a framework that is dynamic, which is going to help in interpreting this kind of analysis.

There are a few methods that go under the idea of dimension reduction and those are known as User Defined Composites and Factor Analysis and Principal Component Analysis.

Clustering

Another method that we need to take some time to explore is known as clustering. This is a technique of machine learning that is able to group different data points into a set of data that is similar. A programmer is often going to use this type of algorithm because it is able to take all of the points of data that they are using and will group them together into groups that fit them the best.

The variables or the points of data that end up going into the same group need to be able to bear some similarities to one another. But the variables that are found in different groups shouldn't be alike at all. This needs to happen as much as possible. Clustering is known as one of the unsupervised machine learning algorithms and it is often used when it is time to work with an analysis of a lot of statistical data.

Data scientists often like to use this kind of analysis of clustering in order to get some better insights into all of the data they have. if you have millions of points of data, it is hard to compute them all and understand what each one means and how it is going to be able to influence what you know and what you do with your points. But when you work with clustering, all of the information is going to be put into different groups (The number of groups will depend on how much data you have and how you can divide it up), and it will help you to read the information better than before.

There are a few different types of clustering that you are able to work with depending on the kind of information that you need to cluster, how many categories you would like it split into, and more. Let's take a look at a few of these and see what they are all about and when you would use them.

K-Means

The K-Means clustering algorithm is one of the first ones that we are going to take a look at here. This one comes with the concept that every data scientist and engineer and anyone else who uses machine learning needs to know how to use it to get the right results. This is one that you really should learn more about because it is easy to add into your code and will ensure you are able to get the results that you would like.

The K-means algorithm is going to start the process by selecting the number of classes and the groups that you want to use. You will also need to come up with an idea of where the center points of these groups will be. If you are starting out with a lot of data and you are not sure how many classes should be used, you can look through the data and see if you can get some ideas. You can also mess around with this a bit and experiment until you find the right number that seems to work for you.

The algorithm is then going to get to work trying to classify what the points of data are. It is able to do this by calculating the distance between the point and all of your center points. The programmer is then able to take a look at this distance and use it in order to categorize the data point in the class whose center is the closest to that point.

Using these classified points that you just figured out, the algorithm is then going to be able to compute where the center of the points is in the class, by utilizing the mean.

The programmer then needs to go through these steps a few times. It is going to continue doing this until the center of the groups does not change between the different iterations that you decide to do. You can also go through and try to initialize the centers in the groups at random, and then select an iteration that is going to give you the best results overall.

K-means is a clustering algorithm that you may need to use on a regular basis. It has the advantage that it is so simple and fast to use, so it makes it really easy to use as a beginner since you are going to be able to use it in a way to compute the distance between the variables and the center of the group. It provides a good and fast way to organize the information that you have.

Of course, there are going to be a few disadvantages that are going to come with this option. First, you need to be able to accurately select the number of classes that you want to add into this simply by looking at the data. And if you have a ton of data, you may find that this is not ideal. And since you may want to find some insight about the data that you are using, it isn't ideal either. And since there are going to be some times when you will need to be random in how you select the center points that you use in the groups, this may cause you to come up with different results for each iteration.

If you want a method that is simple and easy to use, and can help to separate out your data points pretty well, then this method is going to be a great one that you should try out. With that said, there are going to be some times when you are not going to like working with this.

You have to look at your data and figure out whether or not this is the right option for you.

Mean Shift Clustering

Another type of clustering that you may choose to work with is known as the mean shift clustering. This is going to be something that a programmer is able to use when they want to figure out and look through the dense areas that show up in their set of data. This algorithm is also useful because it will take a look at the center points of every group.

However, the main goal that you are going to see with this kind of algorithm is that it is able to do some updates to some of the possible center points of the class within the sliding windows to locate the center point that you want. This can make it a bit better than the K-Means that we talked about before.

This mean shift clustering algorithm is going to remove the points that it chose for the center after it has gotten to the processing stage because this helps it to reduce some of the duplicates that can sometimes form. And once it does this, the algorithm is going to move on to forming the final set of cluster points and placing them in their groups.

Let us first take a look at how this is going to look. Let us consider a set of points in a two-dimensional space. The first step that we need to take here is to define the point around which the circular sliding window is positioned. This window is going to have a radius of r called the kernel. This algorithm is going to be a hill-climbing algorithm and it is constantly going to move the kernel to denser regions until the values are able to converge and come together.

Going back to this sliding window, it is going to continue to move to a denser region at every iteration. The algorithm is able to do this by shifting the center point of all the groups until you get the point that shows up at the mean. The density of the points in this window is going to be proportional to the number of data points that are found inside of it. So, if there are more points in this, this means that the density is going to be higher as well.

What this all means for you is that when you see a shift in the algorithm, it means that the mean of the point in the window is going to start moving over to the areas where the data seems to be denser than the other places.

This sliding window is going to keep on moving according to the change that shows up in the mean. The direction is not going to matter. It just depends on where the mean ends up in all of this. The algorithm will then continue going through all of these steps, working with sliding windows that always change, until it is able to categorize all of the points of data that are found in the set into different sliding windows.

If you do decide to use this method, you will not have to select the number of clusters or classes, which is one of the best advantages that come with this. It is also good that the center points are going to converge together using a mean, and it moves to the mean that is found in the area that is the densest out of all of them. This is because this kind of algorithm is going to really understand the data, and it will try to fit it into any application that is driven by data. The selection of the kernel is not going to be as important with this one, but that, in some cases, is a major drawback that starts to occur.

If you are a beginner with the whole idea of machine learning and the clustering algorithms, then working with the K-means algorithm is going to be the best bet. But once you have a good understanding of how this method works and whether you will be able to use it for your needs or not, you will be able to try out the other algorithms for clustering to help make your analysis a bit better.

Working with Regression Modeling

Now that we have taken some time to explore what the world of clustering is all about in machine learning, it is time to move it a bit further and talk about regression modeling. This is an algorithm that is going to be used if the programmer would like to be able to estimate the values of continuous target variables. There are going to be a variety of regression models that you are able to choose from, but one of the simplest forms of this that you can use is going to be the linear regression model.

With the **linear regression model**, the algorithm is going to try and define the relationship that happens between a continuous predictor variable and a continuous response variable using a straight line. There are going to be models that can use more than one of these variables for predicting things in order to define the response of the variable.

Apart from the models that we already mentioned, there are going to be two other algorithms that can fit with this. These are called the logistic regression methods and the least squared regression. However, there are going to be some assumptions that come with these models can create some disparities. It is important that if you use this one a bit, you are going to need to validate the assumptions that you have before you write out the algorithm and before you even think about building the model.

If you have an engineer that will build up a model and they use it without verifying the assumptions, then you have to be aware of the fact that you will get an output and you won't be able to use it since the model may have failed without the knowledge of the engineer.

When the programmer does get the result, they need to go through and check that there isn't going to be a linear relationship that shows up between the different variables of the models. There are going to be times when the set of data is going to have some variables that may be hidden with the linear relationship that they have. However, there is going to be a systematic approach known as inference, which the programmer can use in order to determine the kind of linear relationship that is present.

We need to take a look at some of the inference methods that the programmer is able to use in order to determine the kind of relationship. Some of the best inference methods that you are able to use includes:

- The t-test. This is going to be used in order to help you know the relationship between your two variables, the predictor and the response.

- The confidence interval for the slope that shows up.

- The confidence interval for the mean of the response variable given a value of the predictor.

- The interval for the prediction that works for your random value of the response variable, given a value of the predictor.

The methods that are described above are going to often depend on the assumption that the programmer decides to make at the beginning of the process. It is easy for the programmer to assess whether the data is able to stick with your assumptions. You are able to check your assumptions with two main graphical methods. You will be able to do a plot of the standardized residuals and the plot of the normal probability.

A normal probability plot is going to be a quantile to quantile plot of the quantiles of distribution against the quantiles of a standard normal distribution for the purposes of determining whether the distribution is going to deviate from what is seen as the normal or the mean. When you work with this kind of plot, the programmer is going to be able to make some comparisons between the value that they observe for the distribution of interest, and compare it to the expected number of values that seem to occur with a distribution that is seen as normal.

If the programmer goes through and does this, the bulk of the points in the plot should end up falling on or near a straight line. If there is a deviation from this kind of plot, it is going to be seen as a deviation. A programmer is then able to validate their assumptions for the regression by seeing what patterns are going to show up on their plat. If they do notice a pattern is showing up, then the programmer is able to identify which assumptions don't seem to hold true very that well. However, if there isn't a pattern that shows up, then the assumptions can stay intact.

If you are taking a look through the graphs and they indicate that there is some violation of the assumptions you made, you may be able to apply a transformation to the response variable y, such as the ln (natural log or the log to the base of e) transformation. If the relationship between the response variables and the variables used for prediction, then the algorithm can be used for transformation.

Gaussian Mixture Models

The next thing that we are going to talk about is known as the Gaussian mixture models. This is a form of density estimation that you are able to use, and can help to give you an approximation of the probability distribution of your data. You are going to choose this kind of model when you notice that the data you are using is multi-modal. This means that there are going to be more than one bump or mode in the histogram. If you remember what we talked about with probability, the mode is simply the values that are the most common.

So the Gaussian mixture will basically be the sum of the weighted Gaussians. To represent these weights, we're going to introduce a brand new symbol that we need called pi. We are going to say pi(k) is the probability that your x value is going to belong to the kth

Gaussian. Since pi(k) is a probability, there is going to be a constraint that all the pi's need to have a sum of 1. If this is confusing, another method that you can think of is that we introduced a new latent variable that is called "z." "Z" is going to represent which Gaussian the data was coming from. So we can basically say pi(k) = P(z=k).

It is similar to saying that there is some hidden cause that is called "z" that we don't know about and we aren't able to measure from the beginning. But each of the "z"s is causing a new Gaussian to be generated, and we will be able to see that the data we place into the system is going to be the combined effects of those individual "z"s.

Training with the GMM is pretty similar to the k-means algorithm that we used earlier, which will make it a bit easier to learn. There are two main steps that you will be able to use to figure out the Gaussian, and they will be similar to what you use with the k-means.

The first step is to calculate the responsibilities. For this one, r(k,n) is going to be the responsibility of the kth Gaussian for generating the nth point. So it's just the proportion of that Gaussian, and then divide it by all of the Gaussians. You can see that if pi(k) is larger here, then it is going to be able to overtake the other Gaussians, and it should be about the value of 1. The algorithm that you would use for this one includes:

r(k,n) = pi(k)N(x(n), mu(k), C(k)) / sum[j=1..K]{pi(j)N(x(n), mu(j), C(j)) }

When working with the C(k), this is going to mean the covariance of the kth Gaussian. The N9x, mu, C) means the probability density function) of your Gaussian of the data point x and the mean mu and covariance C.

Once you have done this part, it is time to move on to step number two. This step is to go through and recalculate all of the parameters of your Gaussians. This means the pi's, covariances, and the means. The method for going through and doing this is going to be pretty similar to what we did with the k-means, where we are going to weigh the influence of each sample on the parameter by using the responsibility. If the responsibility of the sample is small, this means that the "x" is going to matter less in the total of the calculation. Let's look at how we would go through and do this.

Define: $N(k)$ as $N(k) = \text{sum}[n=1..N]\{ r(k,n)\}$

Then each of the parameter updates will be the following:

$mu(k) = \text{sum}[n=1..N]\{ r(k,n)x(n) \} / N(k)$

$C(k) = \text{sum}[n=1..N]\{ r(k,n)(x(n) - mu(k))(x(n) - mu(k))\} / N(k)$

$pi(k) = N(k) / N$

These are just a few of the different algorithms that you are able to use when it comes to working with machine learning. As you read through this book, you can start to see there are a lot of different options when it comes to working with machine learning. And often it is going to depend on what use you have for it from the beginning. If you want to be able to look through and sort through all of the data you have, you may use one algorithm but if you want to guess what products your past customers are going to use and purchase in the future, then the algorithm you use is going to be different.

And that is the beauty of working with machine learning. You will find that because there are already so many applications for working with machine learning, and it is likely that it is going to continue to grow, these numerous learning behaviors are going to be necessary.

Chapter 6

Six: Tips to Make Machine Learning Work for You

Now that we have spent some time to take a look at machine learning and all of the great learning algorithms that fit into the mix, along with the different categories that come with supervised, unsupervised, and reinforcement learning, it is time to move on to actually putting these to use. There are so many different situations where you are able to utilize what you know from machine learning, and it is going to really make a difference if you are able to work on these algorithms.

Once you have a good understanding of these algorithms, you may be more curious about some of the tips and strategies that you are able to use in order to make sure that machine learning is going to work out the way that you would like. Some of the tips that you can follow when it comes to working with machine learning include:

Remember the Logistics

When you are working on machine learning, remember that success is not always just about picking out the right kind of algorithm or tool. In fact, it takes a bit more for this. You need to find a good fit and a good design for the specific kind of problem or project that you want to work with. Each project is going to be different and if you try to use the same things for each one, then there are going to be situations where machine learning will not be successful.

For example, the machine learning that you use with a campaign for online marketing is going to be a lot different compared to working with an algorithm that helps guide an autonomous car. Expanding your resources for an incremental algorithm improvement is going to be really worth it when it comes to the car, but in most marketing cases, you would want to optimize the different logistics around you instead.

This means that before you even get started on the project that you would like to use, you need to take some time to figure out the kind of logistics that are going to make the most sense for what you want to do. We talked about a lot of different algorithms that we can use based on the kind of project or program that you would like to focus on. And each of them presented us with something that was a bit different. Learning how to make these work and picking the right one for the job is important to getting the results that you want.

Mind the Data

Another option that we need to pay attention to is the data that you are going to put through the algorithm. One of the biggest considerations to making sure that all the algorithms you use deliver insights that are valuable is that you have to feed it the right kind of data. If you find that you are running data through an algorithm and the results are not coming out the way you think they should, then it is most likely the data you are using is not right, rather than the algorithm.

There are a lot of programmers or business owners who are going to get all ego-bound and wound up, being stuck to one particular algorithm. But with all of the different tools out there, there is the possibility for way too many new algorithms. While choosing the right algorithm is indeed important to the whole process, the thing that is even more important here is making sure that you are choosing the right kind of data to help you out.

If you are studying with a harder or more complex problem like speech recognition or even something like computer vision, then that is one thing. But this field, despite what we may think when we get a bit lost in it, is that we are in a field that is data-driven. In most of the scenarios that we are going to find ourselves in, making some adjustments to the data that we put in rather than the algorithm is going to make a difference.

Any time that the algorithm is not providing you with the results that make sense or the results that you should be getting when you give it a try, then it is time to make some changes. Maybe you are putting in too much data, or the wrong kind of data, or even not enough data. Changing things around a bit and seeing what that does to the predictions you get may be just the change that you are looking for.

Algorithms Are Not Always Right

We spent a lot of time in this book taking a look at the various algorithms that you are able to focus on. These are great tools that are going to help you to get the right results that you want, but they are not always right. If we start to look at them as magic bullets that are going to solve all of our problems instantly, then this could be a bad thing.

Implementations of machine learning are going to do their very best when there is a continual process of trial and error. No matter how good you may think the algorithms you use are if the system is doing any kind of interaction with another person or several people, then it has to have some adjustments done to it over time. Businesses need to always be measuring the effectiveness of their implementation and figure out if there are any variables and changes that are going to either make it better or make it worse.

This is going to sound like a lot of work and may seem a bit confusing when you are first getting into the field of machine learning. It important, though, and very few businesses are doing this. Instead, they assume that their algorithm is perfect and that it never needs to be changed. This is going to make things worse, and over time, the algorithm is going to be so far behind that it is not going to be able to give you accurate results.

It is normal to want to deploy your system with an algorithm and then want it to do its job perfectly, without ever having to do any work to keep it that way. While that would be the ideal world, that is not a reality that any of us can count on. No algorithm or user interface design is going to be able to stick around and work perfectly for a long time. And there is no data collection method that is going to be superseded.

That means that no matter what kind of algorithm you decide to go with, it is going to need some tune-ups and adjustments over time. If you keep up with this and don't let it fall to the side, then it is likely that the adjustments are going to be small and won't require a ton of work on your part to complete. The biggest issues are going to come when you start to ignore this step, and then the issues start to compound on each other. Remember that no algorithm, no matter how great it may seem, is going to be perfect and you do need to check on it on occasion.

Pick out a toolset that is diverse

There are many different tools available to you and many of them are free! This allows you to have access to countless different resources available to help you get started.

But with this in mind, don't let yourself get glued to one tool. You may have one that is your favorite and that you want to use all of the time. But in reality, when you are working with machine learning, you will really need to bring out several to make this successful. If there is someone around who is trying to convince you that one tool is the only one that is going to work and that you don't need any of the others, then it is time to move away from them and learn about all of the other tools that are really out there.

The neat thing about machine learning is that it is growing like crazy and there are so many people who are interested in learning more about it and using it for their own needs. This is good news for you because there are going to be a lot of different tools available. Experiment with a few and figure out which ones are the best for you. And consider the fact that you are going to need to use a few of these in order to help you to get the work done.

Try Hybrid Learning

Another thing that you can work with is the idea of hybrid learning. You are able to mix together some deep learning with some cheap learning to come up with a hybrid. One example of this is that you are able to take a vision model on a computer that is already in existence and then re-construct the top few layers, the layers that are going to contain the decision that you want to be made. From there, you are able to co-opt a framework already exists, and then use it for a new case.

This is a great way for you to really make something new, without having to create the whole thing from the very beginning. You are able to use some of the techniques and frameworks that are already in existence, and then add some of the specifications and more that are present in it to get the results that you would like.

This can take a bit of work. But think through some of the projects that you want to work with. Break it up into some smaller parts and figure out whether there are any existing platforms or frameworks that you are able to use to get things started. Once you have this, you will be able to go through and make the changes that are needed, perhaps using some of the algorithms that we already have in place and talked about above, to make this happen.

The frameworks that you are going to be using are free in most cases or inexpensive. This means that you will be able to use them and save money compared to recreating exactly what you want from scratch. It is always a good thing in business when you are able to save money. You still get to use the deep learning that is needed in the process, but you get the benefit of saving money on the parts that don't necessarily need to be unique.

Another benefit here is that you can save yourself some time. Many of the frameworks that you are going to use take a lot of time to create. And if you have to come up with a new one each time it is going to take forever to get projects done. When you are able to use or purchase the one that you would like, you can end up saving a lot of time and it speeds up your project.

Remember That Cheap Doesn't Mean That Something Is Bad

This is something that a lot of businesses and programmers are going to run into. We assume that when something is considered cheap (or free) that it is not going to be a good option. Perhaps, you looked at the last tip and cringed a bit because you do not want to work with something that is seen as cheap because you view it as something that is bad.

Despite the connection that has been formed between the word cheap and being bad, this is not the case when it comes to machine learning. The amount of time that you are going to spend on one of the implementations that you want to work with machine learning is not going to necessarily correlate to the amount of value that comes to your business.

The quality that is going to be a bit more important here is to ensure that whatever process you decide to go with is reliable and repeatable. If you are able to achieve this in your business without having to invest too many resources or time, then this is even better. It saves you time, money, and other resources, while still providing you with a huge amount of benefit in the process.

Always remember, when it comes to machine learning that cheap doesn't mean bad. If the learning works, then it works and it doesn't matter if it is cheap. You want to focus your attention on helping your customers or getting the program done, not on how much the program may have cost you along the way. If you need to spend a bit more to get the right tools or the algorithm to work, then go ahead and do it. But if you are able to do it for less, then why waste time and money on something that costs you more.

Never try to call it AI

We talked about this one a bit before. But never confuse AI with machine learning. Businesses need to make sure that they are using the right kind of terminology to ensure that they are getting the most out of this process. You can call these things deep learning, computer vision, or machine learning; but do not call it AI. All of these do sometimes find themselves under the umbrella of artificial intelligence as a term, but they are different.

One of the best ways that you are able to take a look at AI and really understand it is that, right now, it is all of the things that we are not able to explain and talk about yet or the things that data scientists are not able to figure out yet. Before you have been able to figure something out, we are going to call it AI.

This is definitely not going to be machine learning. You want to make sure that you are keeping the two separated. This will ensure that you are able to use machine learning in the proper manner and that you are going to get the most that you can out of these algorithms.

Try Out A Few Different Algorithms

If you want to make the best decisions based on the information and the project that you are trying to work with, you want to make sure that you are working with a few algorithms. When something merges together between the two, then you have a good idea that you have the best prediction for your needs.

We spent some time talking about some of the different types of machine learning. That means that we have a variety of algorithms that go with each category. When you are working with the project or program that you want to create, one of the logical first steps that you should focus on is figuring out which type of machine learning you will need to make the process run smoothly.

Whether you are going to work with supervised machine learning, unsupervised machine learning, or reinforcement machine learning, it is going to direct you to the algorithms that are most likely to work for your needs. If you have no clue what kind of program or problem you need to solve, then it becomes even harder to figure out the best way to solve it and get the results that you want.

Once you have divided your particular problem up based on the type of machine learning that it is; it is time to divide things up even more and figure out which algorithms are going to work the best for the desired results. Maybe there is one learning algorithm that seems to stick out as the best choice, but try to aim for two or three if possible. This may seem like a lot of work, but it is going to really make a difference in the kind of results that you are able to get.

First, you want to try out each of the algorithms that you choose for that set of data based on the category of machine learning that you are working with, and then you want to be able to write down the predictions or the results that you are able to get. If you find that there are some similar predictions that show up between the different algorithms or the algorithms start to show one prediction that stands out from the others and you agree on this prediction, then this is the one that you want to use for your needs.

Working with machine learning can be really exciting. It is going to help you to learn how to sort through some of the data sets that you have available, and it is going to make a big difference in the types of programs that you are able to create along the way. When you are just getting started with machine learning, make sure to check out this guide and learn some of the steps that you are able to take to turn this work into something that makes a world of difference in your program.

Conclusion

The next step is to take a look at the different types of machine learning, and then decide which one is going to work the best for your needs. There are so many different aspects that come with machine learning, and I sincerely hope that you were able to find the information that you need to help you get started with this kind of programming.

You will find that working with machine learning is going to be a bit different than what you did with the traditional coding languages that you may have worked with in the past. This is what makes it more entertaining and fun, and it certainly doesn't mean that the process is going to be more difficult. You will be amazed at all of the complex tasks that you are able to work on, with the simplicity of machine learning.

Thank you for taking the time to read this guide. I know it was a long one, but machine learning is not a five-minute wonder and there is no way that you would grasp any real knowledge of machine learning in just a few thousand words.

Throughout this guide we've covered as much as possible to give you the basics in machine learning, the topics that you need to know and, from here, it's up to you to take your learning further and to put what you learned into practice.

In closing, follow this quick checklist to get you through any machine Learning Project you opt to take on:

- Framing – work out the scope and look at the project as a whole

- Get your data

- Get insights from your data

- Prepare your data so the algorithms can see the data patterns

- Explore models and compare the best ones

- Fine-tune and put your models together in a fantastic solution

- Present that solution

- Launch it

Resources

http://openclassroom.stanford.edu/MainFolder/CoursePage.php?cou rse=MachineLearning

https://azure.microsoft.com/en-us/services/machine-learning-service

https://developers.google.com/machine-learning/crash-course

https://machinelearningmastery.com/machine-learning-in-python-step-by-step/

https://www.edx.org/learn/machine-learning

https://www.ml.cmu.edu

https://www.sas.com/en_us/insights/analytics/machine-learning.html

https://www.udemy.com/machinelearning

MACHINE LEARNING

---

*Master Machine Learning
for Business Leaders*

MG Martin

Introduction

Machine learning has changed the computing world through its digital interactions because it is a form of artificial intelligence. Machine learning begins with data or observations, like instructions or direct experience, and then looks for patterns in the data that allow the machine to make better decisions based on the examples that have been provided. The main aim of machine learning is to allow the machine to learn automatically without any human assistance or intervention and learn to adjust accordingly.

Arthur Samuel coined the term machine learning in the year 1959. However, it was Tom Mitchell who provided a more widely quoted and more formal definition of the various algorithms studied under the field of machine learning. This definition is: *"A computer program is said to learn from experience E with respect to some class of tasks T and performance measure P if its performance at tasks in T, as measured by P, improves with experience E."*

This definition basically offers a fundamental operational version of the term instead of defining it cognitively. Alan Turing proposed in his papers the query "Can machines think?" to be replaced by "Can a machine do what we can do?". Humans can do certain things as thinking entities. The Turing proposal exposes the various characteristics that may be possessed by machines that think.

Allowing computers to learn from their experience means a lot of automation and data analysis of analytical model building by using several algorithms. The machine learning empowers the machines to search and identify concealed insights, without being automated, to look for them when exposed to new data. Although the technology is not that novel, it is gaining momentum as there are a number of things to learn and know about machine learning, often referred to as ML. The various factors responsible for the resurgent interest in ML are affordable computational processing, growing volumes of data sets and affordable storage options for data. Modern-day companies can make an educated decision about developing analytical models by using ML algorithms as they uncover trends, patterns, and connections with minimal human interference.

Machine Learning Evolution

Machine learning in the modern world is different than it used to be. This is mainly due to the emergence of new technologies. In earlier times, the technology gained momentum due to the pattern recognition and the point that the computer didn't have to be programmed to learn and work on certain tasks. There were many scientists who were keen on artificial intelligence who investigated this aspect further to experiment with whether or not computers could learn from the data. The focus was not on iterative learning, as the computers began to adapt to the new data they were being given over a time period. Built on the various patterns and computations they had made in the past, the computers learned to make decisions that were similar to the ones made in the past in the same or similar situations. This capability of the machines to learn from existing patterns is getting massive momentum these days.

People are now sitting up and taking note of the fact that machines are able to apply difficult mathematical calculations to different areas, such as handling large data, and at a much faster rate. Look at the example of the Google car for instance. It is built on machine learning principles. Another significant use of ML can be found in the recommendations used by companies such as Amazon and Netflix, which are an examples of machine learning in our daily lives. ML can also be pooled with the creation of linguistic rules. Twitter currently implements this application, so that you will know what clients are saying about you. More significantly, machine learning is being used to detect fraud in various industrial sectors.

Gone are the days in which the programmers would tell the computer how to resolve an issue at hand. We have reached an era when the machines are left to resolve the issues on their own. They identify the pattern from each data set. Analyzing the hidden patterns and trends makes it simple to guess the future problems as well and also stop from them re-occurring. The machine learning algorithms normally follow a certain kind of data and they use the patterns in the data to answer the queries. For example, you show the machine a series of photographs of dogs and say, "This is a dog." and later show the machine other photos saying, "This is not a dog." Now if you show photographs to the computer it will be trying to identify whether or not the photographs are that of a dog. However, every correct or incorrect guess made by the machine is stored in its memory. This makes the machine smarter in the long run and enriches its knowledge over a time period.

The Significance of Machine Learning in the Modern Business World

Most organizations dealing with a large amount of data have realized the importance of machine learning. By using the hidden insight from this data businesses can work more efficiently and can also acquire a competitive spirit. Apart from bringing about affordable and simple computational processing, it also brings cost-effective storage options. Machine learning has made it feasible to create models that accurately and quickly process and analyze a massive amount of complex data. Along with making it possible for companies to analyze trends and patterns from a range of data sets, ML is also capable of automating the analysis process. This used to be done by humans, slowly. The companies can now deliver personalized services along with differentiated products that cater to the various requirements of the clients, and does it accurately. ML is also helpful to organizations in identifying opportunities that can be lucrative to them in the long run. When you are planning to create an effective machine learning system to increase your business, then here is what you need to do:

- Have knowledge of fundamental and advanced algorithms.

- You must possess great data preparation capabilities.

- Have scalability.

- Have knowledge of Ensemble Modeling.

- Be ready for iterative and automation processes.

As a leader a business leader machine learning is your ticket to advancing your company beyond the competition. Machine learning will help you target your audience, keep your customers happy, and help out money in your bank account.

Chapter 1

Machine Learning for Your Business

Machine Learning and Predictive Analytics

For several companies, huge data - really big volumes of unstructured, semi-structured and raw structured data, is an untapped source of information that can aid business decisions and improve operations. As this data continues to change and diversify, more and more companies are taking to predictive analytics to tap the source and benefit from the large-scale data.

There is a common miscomprehension that machine learning and predictive analytics are one and the same. That is not the case. They do overlap in one area, however, and that is predictive modeling. Basically, predictive analytics includes a range of statistical techniques including ML, data mining and predictive modeling and uses historical and current statistics for estimating or predicting future outcome. This outcome could be the behavior of a customer during the purchase or probable changes in the market. It helps us to guess the possible future occurrences with the analysis of past pattern.

Working of Predictive Analytics

Predictive modeling drives predictive analytics. It is an approach rather than a process. ML and predictive analytics go hand-in-hand because the predictive models typically include ML algorithms. The created models can be trained over a period of time to react to new values or other data thereby delivering the results needed by the organization.

There are two kinds of predictive models. One is the classification model, which predicts class membership and the second is the regression model that predicts numbers. The models are made from algorithms that perform data mining and statistical analysis to determine patterns and trends in the data. The predictive analytics software will have built-in algorithms that can be used to create predictive models. Algorithms are known as classifiers and they identify the set of categories to which the data belongs.

Commonly Used Predictive Models

The most widely used predictive models are:

- *Regression (Linear and Logistic)*: It is one of the more popular methods available in statistics. Regression analysis provides a relationship between variables and finds key patterns in diverse and big data sets. It also finds out how they relate to each other.

- *Decision Trees*: The decision trees are simple yet powerful forms of multiple variable analysis. Decision trees are produced by algorithms that identify different ways of splitting the data into branch-like segments. They partition the data into subsets depending on various categories of input variables. It helps you understand a user's path to a decision.

- *Neural Networks*: They are built on the patterns of the neurons in the human brain. Neural networks are often referred to as artificial neural networks and are a variance of deep learning technology. They are commonly used to solve difficult pattern recognition situations and are unbelievably useful for analyzing big data sets. They are very good at handling nonlinear data relationships and also work well when some variables are unknown.

Classifiers

Every classifier approaches the data in a different manner, so for the managers to get the results they require, they must select right classifiers and models.

- *Clustering algorithms*: They organize data into different groups with similar members.

- *Time Series algorithms*: They plot the data sequentially and are useful in forecasting constant values over a period of time.

- *Outlier Detection algorithms*: They focus completely on anomaly detection, identifying events, observations or items that don't conform to a specific expected pattern or standards in a data set.

- *Ensemble Models*: These models make use of several ML algorithms for obtaining a better predictive performance than compared to the output expected from a single algorithm.

- *Naive Bayes*: This classifier permits you to predict a category or a class based on a provided set of features by using probability.

- *Factor Analysis*: It is a method used for describing variations and aims at finding independent latency in variables.

- *Support Vector Machines*: They are a supervised kind of machine learning technique that uses associated learning algorithms for analyzing data and recognizing patterns.

Machine Learning and Predictive Analytics Applications

The companies that are overflowing with data are struggling to turn all the information into useful insight. For these organizations, ML and predictive analytics can provide the solution. No matter how big the data is, if it cannot be used to enhance the external and internal processes and meet objectives, it becomes a useless resource. Predictive analysis is used more commonly in marketing, security, risks, fraud detection and operations. Here are some of the examples of how machine learning and predictive analytics are used in various industries,

- *Financial Services and Banking*: In the financial services and banking industry, ML and predictive analytics are used together to measure market risks, detect and decrease fraud, identify opportunities and there are several other uses.

- *Security*: Cyber security is at the top of the agenda for almost all businesses in the modern world. It is no surprise that ML and predictive analytics play a key role in security aspects. The security organizations use predictive analysis often to improve their performance and services. They can detect anomalies, understand client behavior, detect fraud and as a result, they enhance data security.

- *Retail*: The retail industry is using ML for understanding customer behavior better. Who is buying what and where? They want to know the answer to these queries. These questions can be answered with accurate predictive models and data sets thereby helping retailers to plan beforehand and stock items based on consumer trends and seasonality. Improves the ROI a great deal.

Developing the Right Environment

Although predictive analytics and ML can be a huge boost for most companies, implementing these solutions halfheartedly without consideration for their fitment into everyday operations will only hinder their potency to deliver the insight the company needs. To get the best out of ML and predictive analytics, companies need to make sure that they have the architecture to support the solutions along with high-quality data that will help them in learning. Data preparation and its quality are the key portions of predictive analytics.

The input data, which may span across several platforms and consist of multiple data sources, needs to be centralized and unified in a coherent way. To achieve this, the companies need to develop good reliable data governance programs to govern the overall data management and make sure that only the high-quality data gets captured and used. In addition, the current processes might have to be altered to include ML and predictive analytics, as this will enable companies to have efficiency at all points of the business. And most importantly the companies must know what issues they want to be resolved, as it will aid them in determining the most suitable model for use.

Predictive Models

The IT experts and data scientists working in an organization are normally tasked with selecting or developing the right predictive models or possibly build one for themselves to satisfy the organization needs. However, these days the ML and predictive analytics is not just the area of expertise for mathematicians, data scientists, and statisticians, but there are business consultants and analyst working in the area. More and more people in businesses are using the models to develop insights and improve operations. However, there are issues when they are not aware of what model to use or how to deploy it or in the case when they need some information immediately. There is sophisticated software available to help the employees with the problem.

Chapter 2

Machine Learning and Data Mining

Data mining means extracting knowledge out of huge quantities of data. In other words, we can say that it is a process of discovering different kinds of patterns inherited in the data sets that are new, useful and accurate. Data mining is an iterative process that creates descriptive and predictive models by uncovering previously unknown patterns and trends in a large quantity of data. This exercise is executed to support decision making. It is basically a subset of business analytics and is similar to experimental research. Origins of data mining can be found in statistics and databases. ML, on the other hand, works with algorithms that improve automatically via experience they gain out of data. In other words, in machine learning, we discover new algorithms from experience. These algorithms of ML can extract information automatically, but the source used for machine learning is also data. It involves two kinds of data: one is test data and the second is the training data. Data mining techniques are commonly used in machine learning and along with the learning algorithms it is used to build models of what is happening behind the scenes to predict the outcome of the future.

What is data mining and what is the relationship between ML and data mining? Data Mining means extracting knowledge out of a big amount of data. It was introduced in 1930 and at first it was referred to as knowledge discovery in database. Data mining is utilized to get rules out of existing data. Its origins lie in conventional databases having unstructured data. It is implemented where you can develop your own models and the data mining techniques are used. It is more natural and involves more involvement of human beings. They are used in cluster analysis. Data mining is abstracted from data warehousing. It is more of a research using methods similar to ML but is applied in limited sectors.

Data Mining Techniques

The specialists working in the field of data mining rely on techniques and intersection of statistics, database management, and machine learning. They have dedicated their careers to understanding what conclusions are to be drawn from a huge amount of information. What are the techniques used for turning this into reality? Data mining is effective when it draws on some of these techniques for their analysis.

1. *Tracking Pattern*: One of the fundamental techniques used in data mining is learning to recognize patterns in the data sets. Normally this is an aberration in the data that is happening at some interval or a flaw or an ebb in some variables over a period of time. For example, you may observe that sale of certain product spike up immediately before holidays. Or you may notice that warm weather drives people to your site.

2. *Classification*: It is a more complex data mining technique that asks you to collect different attributes together in discernable categories that can be later used to arrive at further

conclusions or serve in some other function. For example, in case you are evaluating the data on independent client's financial background and purchase history you may be able to classify the individuals as high, medium or low-risk candidates for credit. You can then use the classifications to learn more about the clients.

3. *Association*: This is related more to tracking patterns, however, it is more specifically involved in the dependently linked variables. In the case of an association, you look for specific attributes or events that are correlated to other attributes or events. For example, you may notice that when your customer purchases some specific item they also buy another related item. This sequence of events is used to populate the "people also bought" section in the online store.

4. *Outlier Detection*: In some cases, just identifying the overreaching pattern cannot give you a clear understanding of the data set. You are also required to understand the anomalies, also called outliers in the data. For example, your buyers are almost exclusively male, however, during a single week in July there is a sudden rise in female buyers. You may want to investigate the reason for the event and find out what drove the sales so, you can either replicate it or understand the behavior of your audience better.

5. *Clustering*: This is similar to classification, however, involves grouping of chunks of data together which is similar. For example, you may select to cluster different demographics of the customers in various packets based on how much extra income they earn or how often they are shopping at the online store.

6. *Regression*: Regression is used basically as a form of modeling and planning. It is used to find out the chances of presence of certain variables because some other variables are

there. For example, you may use this to project some price based on factors such as consumer demand, competition, and availability. More specifically, the main focus of regression is in helping you uncover exact relationships between two or more variables inside a specific data set.

7. *Prediction*: It is easily one of the most valuable data mining techniques used. This is because it is used for predicting the kind of data you will see in future. In some cases, just by understanding and recognizing the historical trends we can chart an accurate prediction of what will happen in the future. For example, we can see the credit history of clients and their past buys to predict whether there will be a credit risk in future in case a loan is extended.

Business Process Optimization

Optimizing your business involves a process of measuring productivity, efficiency, and performance of your business and finding out methods for improving the measures. It is an act of taking the older business process and optimizing it for quality. However, the means for achieving it differ quite a lot. The business process optimization happens to be one of the last steps used in BPM (Business Process Management). It is a method that advocates a continuous process re-evaluation and improvement. Therefore in order to make it work, you must carry out the first three steps necessary for any BPM initiative. These steps are:

1. *Process identification*: You must already be aware of the process that you need to optimize. In a lot of cases, you will select processes that are critical for the organization and are drivers for the profits. After all, what is the point of performing the optimization if it cannot have any impact?

2. *Business process mapping*: Until you have mapped the business process you will have a difficult time finding out

74

possible improvements. In case you don't map for the business process, you can do it with a flowchart by using just a pen and paper or by using workflow software.

3. ***Business Process Analysis***: Before beginning the improvement activity in a business process you need to analyze every step first. This analysis can either be completely straightforward with some totally obvious possible changes or could be a lot more difficult in case the issues are not so apparent. In case of later, you can make use of some of the tools used for business process improvement to find out the minute inefficiencies.

After completing this, with all that out of the way, you need to have a clearly mapped out and defined process and a few ideas about how to optimize the same.

Executing the Business Process Optimization

There are many methods that can be used for optimizing your business processes. This depends on the process that is selected for optimization. You cannot find one size that will fit the description for all. However, in most cases, the optimization is performed by using one of the following methods.

Re-structuring or Process Improvement: This method is quite simple and it just takes a good look at every step in the process. The idea in this method is to find out the processes that are:

A. Wasteful: Every step in a process must add some value to the end target, which could be some output or certain value. And the process must collect to something in the context of company goals. Many times you will find that some steps or processes are useless without the creation of some value. There are different kinds of wastes and wasteful processes.

B. Inefficient and Improvable: This means that a process or a step is just not as efficient as it may be. For example, there may be a lot more steps being taken than required. One of the most glaring examples of this is the approval processes. In case you are trying to have a new project off the ground, you are required to get approvals from senior management in the company. Meaning you will be required to wait for more than five very busy executives to find time to read documents and provide green light.

Once you have found out the steps or processes that fall into these categories you will be required to improve them for quality. This can be achieved by restructuring the process. In other words. by changing the steps or restructuring the steps by eliminating the useless steps or processes or by doing a bit of both.

Automation

Many people don't like manual work. Many times it makes you feel as if you are a cog in the machine doing things that robots can do better. All you need to do is find the right tools or software for the work. The BPA (Business Process Automation) can help you with taking out manual labor from your employees' workload and this leads to better productivity and morale as the employees will work on what matters. No one likes the grunt work. Automation varies with tasks. Here are some examples of automation:

Customer Support: In case you are working with your business associates online you will have customer support form open on the site. Let's say there is an issue with the new software update and as a result, 10% of the user base is affected. This means your inbox is getting really clogged with emails with complaints and issues. Although the first bug report is very useful, the rest is only a clutter and you have to reply to them all. There is software available that allows you to create events in which case you can send automatic replies to the complaints depending on keywords mentioned in the ticket.

Social Media Management: Whatever the organization is about, the employees will have Facebook accounts in all probability or at least LinkedIn pages. The conventional ways of managing the pages are to have someone log in manually and then find something to post 3-4 times every day. Instead of wasting your time doing all this you can use a social media tool to plan your posts right through the next month.

There are other examples that might be more relevant to your business. But many such solutions are available online to help you out in your business process automation endeavor.

Adopting Technology and Total Process Change

Adopting the correct technology will always be the game changer. Unlike the first two approaches, this doesn't exactly optimize the process as such. Instead, it changes it totally. Let's say that you make use of the whiteboard to organize your daily chores with the organization. By adopting the task management software you can improve the daily efficiency of businesses without actually changing any process. By having software in charge you will see benefits such as:

- *Less mistakes and missed deadlines*: Humans are notorious for making errors. Everyone can mess up once in a while or forget something important or miss a deadline. The task management software ensures that this doesn't happen as it reminds you of the daily tasks and ensuing deadlines.

- *Central Command Center*: It is much easier to create new tasks online and pin them to your employees instead of sending them detailed emails and hope that it doesn't get overlooked or lost.

For more process-oriented examples there is workflow management software available. Rather than having to keep track of workflow manually via chat or email you can use dedicated systems to manage all the processes via a single dashboard. This automatically eliminates many issues you will encounter with process management like;

- *Lack of Standardization in Processes*: It is very difficult to make all your employees follow different procedures at the same time. The workflow software ensures that everyone is completing all the required steps in the process in the correct order.

- *Simpler Tracking and Analysis*: The workflow software allows easier tracking than compared to the average process maps. Without the software, you will need to keep track of the processes manually through email and chat. Additionally the software measures process efficiency as otherwise, you will have to manually gather all the data from different reports, employees and software.

Therefore for optimizing the business processes, you need to identify the weak and inefficient processes, map them out and analyze them. Find out if there are better ways of doing them. Then optimize them by either restructuring them, automating or adopting some technology that will totally change the way things worked.

Optimizing Business Resources

When you are hiring for startups there is a golden rule, recruit only when the existing employees are 120% stretched. Simply put, the startups cannot take employees who cannot be 100% utilized. There isn't any room for excess baggage. Although this makes sense in business terms you can also bring down the moral of the employees by overworking them. The answer is in optimizing the business resources so that it is possible to extract better productivity from the team before starting the recruitment of new people.

a. Value over Volume

One of the fastest and yet more difficult decisions to take for the startup owners is optimization of business resources. It is a difficult decision to have value over volume. It probably means raising the value of the product or services in a way that the volume of transactions comes down but due to the higher margins, the revenue actually goes up. Employees now will have more time to finish their tasks and as a result, can provide a better quality of service to existing clients. All this is easier said than done though and the decisions need to be taken after careful deliberations.

b. Reduce Waste

Waste is a big problem, especially in consumable businesses. Not only does it increase the operational cost but can also overwork and frustrate the employees by forcing them to produce items that might get thrown away eventually. Better prediction models and forecasting tools will aid in optimizing the operations, reducing the workload of employees and increase revenues in the process.

c. Re-engineering the Operations

It is a common practice for startup employees to don many hats at work to take care of different tasks at the same time. Studies have indicated that splitting the attention across several tasks can decrease the productivity and increase the time required to complete every task by as much as 25%. Although having to play multiple roles is a part of the startup business there may still be able to re-engineer operations so that these employees can focus on one thing at a time. For example, in case you have a marketer who looks after all the digital activities you can rearrange their workload by making them focus on email marketing just on a single day of the week.

d. Outsourcing the Non-Value adding work

There is no need to do all the work in-house. Many consulting firms have devoted staffs that are capable of taking care of different tasks such as preparing presentations or aggregating the spreadsheets. Although these tasks are significant, it does not make sense for consultants having high values rates to perform them. Startups can take inspiration from the outsourcing to perform similarly and outsource some tasks to some data processing industry that can take care of all non-value-adding task items and release the company employees from tedious work. These tasks could be trivial, such as submitting taxi receipts for compensation or something more significant such as converting a Word document into PPT for presentation. From the business point of view, it may increase the costs but it also increases the efficiency of your team dramatically. In turn, it helps in accelerating business growth.

e. Using Third-Party Tools

When you are a new business, it is important to focus all resources on the core specialties. It means avoiding working on things that do not directly contribute toward making the product or service better. For example, you may integrate your software with the third party tools that help in achieving some functionalities without the organization having to build the features yourself. Uber is one of the more popular startups in the world and its app still runs on Google Maps. By not working on the mapping portion of their requirement themselves Uber was able to arrive in the market sooner and that has contributed a great deal to their success.

Business optimization rationale in new businesses is pretty simple: the bootstrapped businesses cannot afford inefficiency. The basic rule is to look into every task performed by employees in your company objectively and ask yourself these questions, can this task be scrapped altogether? Can it be outsourced? Can the process be optimized to improve efficiency?

Optimizing Business Operations

Business operations can always be improved for any organization. In fact, honing efficiency and effectiveness is critical for a middle market corporation. You will need all the available resources to encompass the next stage of growth and be capable of managing competition from larger organizations. Instead of working at a smaller scale and keeping on fixing sporadic problems, one is better off at using one of these strategies to address various aspects of the operations. Here are some strategies that will help in shaking loose the operations section and free resources that can be utilized better in some other areas.

Take the "Lean" Approach: An operational philosophy, "LEAN" focuses on improving operational activities continuously so that you deliver products and services to your clients with higher internal and external value. By having practices that cause value addition and avoiding the practices that do not, the company makes its operations department more efficient. There are organizations that have a worksheet to aid executives to determine whether their companies are actually employing lean practices or are only working on some related jargon.

Focusing on Quality: There are several versions of quality management available in business theories for many years like "statistical process control" by W Edwards Deming, the total quality movement of the 1980s or other practices such as six sigma. These practices were originally intended for production but later expanded in operational work of the organizations. The main idea is to reduce work and wastage thereby saving money in the process, improving results and making the organization more effective.

Improving Forecasting: Whether you are selling products or services, buying and managing inventory, controlling supply chains or correctly staffing the company, all organizations try to forecast the demand. Several companies are not very good at forecasting but it only means that they are not prepared to meet the market demands or are wasting money and activities on keeping over capacity. According to the NCMM whitepaper, the bourbon distiller Maker's Mark broadcasted that it will have to water its products because of low-quality forecasting. As they were not able to satisfy their clients they were irate. Luckily for the middle market companies, sophisticated tools are available with extensive knowledge to improve forecasting of all kinds.

Introducing Customer Focused Thinking

The management teams are always fond of saying how customer-centric their organizations are. Match it with your experience as a customer and now think how many organizations place their customers first. The customer-centric approach by any business is unbelievably efficient. In the end, it is the customers and their perception and attitude towards a business that decides its fate. You need to focus your strategy and operations to embrace the customers and keep them satisfied and happy. If you can do that you are on a fast path to success in business.

The Good Old BPR (Business Process Re-engineering)

BPR (Business Process Reengineering at one point of time was a craze among company management. Organizations were trying to rework their operational process to achieve greater efficiency. Similar to all fads, it was a lot of talk and very little action. The idea, however, has not lost its credibility as business processes develop over a period of time. As the conditions change, organizations keep adopting and adding to the processes. In the end, you will have a difficult process going that was designed by a committee. However, with real re-engineering, organizations can isolate the wasteful processes in the running of the business and develop better and more effective processes. During re-engineering, the business processes remember to have the frontline employees involved. They are the ones who actually know how things take place and they might even have inputs on how to make things better.

Research

Performing the right research is essential in predicting the future of your products. There are several methods for researching product trends.

1. *Social Media*: Always keep an eye on the trends that appear on the social media pages. You will find some people behaving and communicating in certain manner as well as make up their minds on some buying options. One example is people posting opinions, content or web links all across the FB walls. Some special social groups are created on different platforms that are active followers of the specific product or industry.

2. *Product Tracking Software*: You will also need to perform some current product sales research before you start predicting the product trends more accurately. For example you can easily find how ASIN is doing by inputting ASIN in the "Trendster". Use the statistics you find along with the insight to develop your understanding of market behavior.

When you have gone through all these resources you would have gathered the information necessary for going to the next step.

Differentiate Between Real Trends and Momentary Crazes

It is important to remember that you are trying to predict product trends and not the momentary fads that hit the market. As the trend can go on for years or even decades while the craze is likely to live for a season at the most. It fades and it is fairly easy to spot the craze in case you consider some factors. The real thing must have the following:

Inherent Utility: Does the specific item serve any useful purpose? Or is it relying on specific circumstances to show its usefulness?

Long-term value: Will people still love the product in a few years? Will it survive the change of season?

Does it mold with other trends? - Does it make sense to use it in a broader context of the industry? As was mentioned before, the trends do not exist in isolation. One example is Acai, which exploded in popularity in the last decade due to the quality it has as an organic super fruit. But it also tastes good. So the Acai trend fits with other trends such as novelty, health and awareness.

Being able to predict the product trends is being a step ahead of the competition. It provides you a priceless opportunity to go to the market with something completely new. Following the steps provides great insight, which refines your understanding of the market and its variance. When you have discovered a trend study it to ensure that it is not just a craze and perform the research. Many sellers make the mistake of assuming that just because a product is popular it will continue to sell highly. But to be certain that you have found a trend, you may want to see other products in the category and how they are doing right now. A quick search online can reveal crucial information about the sales of a specific product. It helps you arrive to accurate conclusions about the trends.

Data-Driven Strategy

In order to ensure that the marketing section is contributing effectively towards the business, you need a customizable data-driven strategy. Data reveals the strengths and weaknesses of all parts of your business thereby allowing you to take strategic decisions to develop a marketing strategy for success. Most marketers feel that data is any company's most underused asset. So how to incorporate data-driven marketing in your business and start enjoying the benefits? Here are some steps you can follow to make sure that you are using data to effectively run the marketing strategy.

1. ***Determine your goals***: There is one important step before you start data collection and that is knowing which data is worth collecting. Decide what kind of data will have a positive impact on the marketing strategy. Leave out the data that will not be used to add the effectiveness of the strategy and focus on collecting data around key KPIs, which can actually move the things along.

2. ***Build your team***: Before beginning to analyze data it is significant to build a team to handle it. The team must include members from various departments and cross-disciplinary sections. Richard Baystom suggested on Effin Amazing that it doesn't mean that someone from IT gets together with someone from sales just collecting the guys the managers can spare. It means that you find people who are willing to go beyond their area of expertise and knowledge. For example, you need data scientists who are willing to learn about marketing or IT people who are willing to learn about sales. Prioritizing the collaboration of these people by scheduling focused frequent meeting is critical. In the meetings, everyone shares their ideas and information and can take the credit when the team is successful.

3. ***Gather the Data***: When you are ready to start gathering the data you need to ensure that you place it in one place for easy analysis. Think about collecting the following kind of data:

   • Competitors

   • Targeted market

   • Marketing

- Social media analytics (impressions, click-throughs, conversions etc.)

- Customer data including personal, transaction data, online activity, and social network activity

- Qualitative and Prospect data

There are even more kinds of data. You can begin by asking the different members of the team what kind of data they prepare and use and gather all kind of information you can from other departments also. Jim Bergeson has pointed out in an article that data is sometimes hidden in the innermost resources of your company, maybe with the vendors or dealers or resellers of the product or services. It could be with the sales people or even locked up in an IT section vault.

Once this data exploration is done you will learn what is happening at all stages of the customer lifecycle with information such as, problems at the sales point, complaints or service calls, referrals, subsequent purchases, and online recommendations.

4. *Evaluating the Data & Taking Action*: Evaluate the collected data against the KPIs and start using this data to drive the marketing strategies.

a. Refine the content marketing strategy:

You may already be using the content marketing strategy to attract and engage the audience. But sometimes there is no clear strategy behind the content or you do not have a clear idea about whom you are trying to reach. However, once you have the data to make educated decisions you are on your way. You can maybe combine the sales and marketing strategies together to make more money. You can also experiment with different kinds of content such as GIFs, images and videos. In case you are already putting out good content regularly this step should not be a problem. However, do not forget the most important part and that is engagement. When you provide your customers what they want they are more likely to be engaged in the content. It will need some trial and error but the data will aid you in determining the best way to engage the audience.

b. Consider new Submarkets:

Once you have all the insight from the collected data you can begin creating new submarkets for your products and services. This doesn't mean that you need to change the brand entirely, perhaps you just need to modify whom you are selling your product to. For example, in case you are currently selling custom signage for the birthday parties and you find out that there is a massive demand for similar products for weddings, you may wish to tweak the marketing strategy a little to target engaged couples and perhaps create a new line for them. The overall target is to look for opportunities in the niche and serve the new audience with your products and services.

c. Removing the Hurdles:

The collected data will also reveal the possible hurdles potential clients are facing in the sales process. This is the time to address these issues. Are your customers getting stuck with the product items in the cart? How can you make them complete the purchase? One of the examples is Pura Vida bracelets. The company promotes the products via content on Facebook and they recently offered a time-sensitive discount for the fan page to motivate the shoppers.

d. Exploring alternative marketing channels:

Sometimes you discover that your business is not reaching all the necessary customers. In case your site is the only channel you are using to share information about your products and services, your business will not sustain. The collected data can help you look into other channels and ways. You might want to try the co-marketing opportunities with other businesses having different products than your own or start an affiliate program in which the high-value customers spread a word about your products in exchange of discounts or some other benefits. By analyzing the collected data you will start to understand what channels are most suitable for your products and services.

e. Do not stop testing:

Although data can aid in the development of new marketing strategies, it needs to be frequently tested and managed. In "New Breed Marketing" Matthew Buckley states that you need to test your marketing efforts with small experiments that can be achieved in a single day. He suggested the use of scientific methods to do so. The target is to gather all the important data quickly and proficiently so that you can carry on drawing conclusions from it and even build new experiments. More the testing you perform on the data more informed is your marketing effort.

Achieving the truly data-driven marketing effort is challenging. A study from CMO Council and RedPointGlobal which is titled "Empowering the Data-Driven Customer Strategy: Addressing Customer Engagement from the Foundation Up" points to four hurdles that will keep the marketers from moving the developed strategies towards execution. The issues include a lack of real-time data, lack of internal cohesiveness, and lack of technology and customer focus. The study describes that only 7% of the marketers are saying that they can always deliver data-driven, real-time experiences across several physical and digital touch points. Although 52% of marketers asserted that they can deliver most of the experiences, they could do so only via digital channels or marketing owned channels. So, in reality, many companies are having trouble in gathering and analyzing data across various channels in real time.

In order to achieve a real triumph in data-driven marketing, businesses need the right kind of technology. One-third of people say that they invested in five out of ten independent platforms or solutions in the last five years, however many still don't have the requisite tools to visualize their data fully. The real issue is the connectivity between the solutions. About 3% of marketers are saying that all their systems are totally in sync thereby connecting all the data, metrics and the insight smoothly across all channels. 15% admitted that they have no strategy at all for the development of internal processes and technologies in order to adopt newer cloud solutions in their legacy infrastructure.

Targeting and Connecting with Potential Customers

In case you are rolling out new marketing plans or are looking to provide a facelift to the current one, here are some ways to help you connect with the customers and foster some leads. Arriving at a right and effective marketing strategy is not an easy task. You need to make decisions about who you think the clients are then spending a huge amount of time collecting and analyzing data about their buying habits. It is both expensive and time-consuming. But this monetary and time-consuming investment may yield results that are game-changing for the organization. If you are beginning to formulate a marketing strategy and netting some customers here are the steps to take for success.

1. *Identify the Customers*: You will not be able to connect positively with your potential clientele in case you do not have the potential clients in mind. Survey the current customers along with members of the targeted market. This is to find out how you may improve your presentation of your products and services or what is missing from what is being offered by you

89

at the moment. Throw a large net to capture people that are interested in your products and services and use their data to develop your brand in a better way to resonate with the targeted market. When you know about the audience, where they hang out on the Internet and what they react to, then you can start marketing.

2. ***Research the competitors to find out their customers***: A simple way to find out the most effective marketing campaign for your products is by researching your competitors. Not only the simple exercise will provide an insight into the ideas for your own campaigns it will reveal the dark areas in the competitor's modus operandi and provide new directions for you. If you are going in a business from the same industry you will eventually compete with the competitor for the same targeted market. So might as well use their example to improve your products and services.

3. ***Targeted Advertisements***: For an economical and yet effective method of advertising, Google and Facebook prove that just a little bit can go a long way. Although most of the advertising in the real world reaches those who come across the billboards, commercials or bus stops, these targeted ads are capable of locating people that are most likely to need your services based on their geographical locations, demographics (such as age, education, gender and status of relationship), browsing activities and interests. With investment in the targeted ads and paying via their PPC (Pay per Click) or PPI (Pay per Impression) methods, the organizations can see significant bumps in user engagements, sales, and most importantly conversion.

4. ***Social Media Use***: There is a huge difference in having a little bit of presence on social media and having the social media presence. When you are trying to keep your customers, a bit more effort on Twitter, Facebook and Instagram go a long way.

Many businesses just use their accounts to only promote their company. But smart social media operators strategize the relevant posts, links to great articles and answer customer queries as soon as they are asked. As a result, they are giving customers the impression that they are human beings who genuinely care. These are the organizations that retain their customers. Provide the users with new ways of using their products or services and help to solve issues as and when they arise.

5. ***Respond to all Communication***: Paul English was leading Kayak and he used one of the most valuable practices ever. He insisted that there was an extremely annoying and loud phone right in the middle of his office. This was for receiving customer complaints. This practically ensured that the calls were answered by everyone including developers, engineers, managers, and by English himself. Tony Hsieh valued the customer service so much that he built a customer service training program for all new hires regardless of their portfolio. His customer service went to such lengths that his people went to a rival shoe shop to get a pair of shoes which were not available on the website. The point is, always answer the calls, take care of your customers and fix problems when they happen. Your clientele will love you for the service.

6. ***Affiliate Marketing***: It has been around since the days when WWW was introduced and yet it still gets overlooked. However, it is extremely effective in raising brand awareness significantly. With a number of affiliate networks operating out there working on PPC or PPA (Pay per Action) basis, it has never been safer and easier to find whether your product is actually being promoted by the appropriate publishers. Amazon, eBay, and some other establishments offer their very own affiliate networks however, you may also try for exclusive PPA affiliate networks.

7. ***Establish Trust in the Community by Publishing Reviews etc.***: There are many new and competitive businesses congesting almost all industries. It is getting more and more difficult to stand and grow in terms of a decent following. In order to gain support, organizations must be able to establish trust. There are as many as 88% of customers who trust online reviews as much as personal recommendations so it is only sensible to start publishing reviews and sending samples of the product for the trusted bloggers to read and judge.

As the company starts to grow, begin placing in-house content on the large websites that publish syndicated content such as Forbes, Huffington Post, Fast Company Inc., and FT. Do not forget to use your real name here as people respond better to humans rather than corporations.

8. ***Connect with Influencers***: Engage with the large player in the industry as it is an effective method for garnering a wide customer base. As, when you can get the attention of an influencer or a thought leader, you have a better chance of capturing their friends and fans as well as establish credibility and trust. Reach out to the entrepreneurs at conferences or bloggers on Twitter or send them interesting and relevant blog content which may raise their interest and again-be human, not just an organization.

9. ***Post Content on Blogs***: Keep the practice of continuously and diligently posting original and relevant blog content. It keeps your organization shining in Google. However, it also helps potential customers to know your company truly and know where it is coming from. This content doesn't have to be all self-promoting, rather it should offer context and insight into why the reader should buy the product or service. Suggest the best methods for solving industry-related issues that appear in the everyday life of your customers or impart some useful information and in general inspire people to share your point of

view. In case you do not have sufficient writers or resources on the payroll to keep out rolling a constant flow of content on the blog, you can enlist to the content marketing platforms such as Content.ly or virtual communication platforms such as Commeta.

10. *Use Newsletters to Foster Leads*: One of the most difficult tasks in online marketing is generating leads. Often this involves analyzing the customer information and social media activities, placing ads, online surveys and yearly updating of user data. However, new companies keep coming up to simplify the lead generation and in some cases do the work for you. One example is LeadGenius. For nurturing prospects, a great method is using personalized email newsletters, promotional campaigns, and A/B test advertising. Use data to fine tune the efforts that are showing results and develop the best possible campaign.

Chapter 3

Machine Learning for Marketing

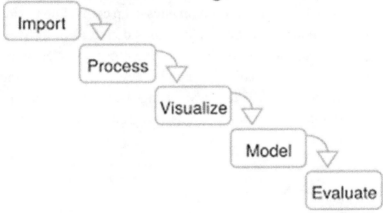

Machine learning workflow

Import → Process → Visualize → Model → Evaluate

Applications for Marketing

Marketing success depends on several factors. Apart from those mentioned above, marketers cannot win without mastering automation and data analytics. Machine learning can improve the performance of common tasks such as generating branded collateral, customer segmentation, customer communication, extraction and classification of relevant content, overall productivity and output. In the modern economy marketing companies without machine learning will be operating with a serious handicap. However, adopting ML without understanding what it can do is likely to cause more harm than benefit (normally expressed in terms of wasted hours and money). It is no magic and will not move the needle automatically unless your team chooses and configures the correct ML solution for particular marketing challenges. Here are some applications using machine learning techniques for marketing:

1. ***Customer Segmentation and Discovery by Clustering***: All your clientele is not the same. The unsupervised ML can aid you to group the audience into dynamic groups and engage them suitably. For example, Affinio's platform analyses billions of customer interest variables, finds the particular customer interests based on their social media activities and then generates visual reports grouping the customers having similar interests. After this, you are able to gain insight on the customer behavior you can identify who is a die-hard foodie, who follows what series on Netflix or who have a liking for similar travel destinations.

2. ***Content Optimization by using Multi-Arm Contextual Bandits***: A/B tests is an effective way of finding out which kind of content (web page layout, email tone, article headlines, and visual elements etc.) resonate better with the audience. But, there is a period of regret in A/B testing where you can lose revenue when you are using less optimal options. You need to wait and finish the countdown till you learn what the best option is. The bandit test, on the other hand, reduces the opportunity loss via dynamic optimization. In the process, it explores and exploits the options simultaneously thereby moving towards the better option gradually and automatically.

3. ***Regression Models with Dynamic Pricing***: The correct pricing can make or break the future of a product. The regression techniques in ML permit marketers to predict statistical values based on previously existing features. This, in turn, permits them to enhance various aspects of the client's journey. Regression can also be utilized for sales forecasting and optimizing marketing expenditure.

4. ***Text Classification for Personalization and User Insight***: A machine learning system can use NLP (Natural Language Processing) to probe voice or text-based content then classify all pieces of the content based on variables like the sentiment, topic or tone to generate customer insight or curate relevant material. The Tone Analyzer from IBM Watson can parse through the customer feedback from the internet and determine the general tone of users that are reviewing the products.

5. ***Text Extraction and Summary for Trending News***: Machine learning can be leveraged by marketers to extract relevant content from news articles published online and other sources of data to determine customer opinions about their brand and how they react to the products. For this the "Protagonist" platform enables organizations to gain complete visibility of their client's motivation and values and how these attributes can affect their purchasing decisions. The technology savvy marketers can also build their own machine learning algorithms by using APIs like AYLIEN for social media sentiment monitoring and relevant news aggregation among other purposes.

6. ***Machine Translation Using Attentional Neural Networks***: The attention mechanisms of deep learning aid in helping improve the machine translation and enrich your marketing assets for global competition. The translation was a major expenditure for a brand entering into a new and linguistically different market. However, the development in the AI field has enabled machine translation to gain near human parity. In order to rationalize the costs and speed up this process, several companies opt to just have human translators review and sign off the output from machine translation.

7. ***Text Generation by using RNN (Recurrent Neural Networks)***: In case the creative people of your brand are under constant pressure to come up with great names for your newer products

and campaigns, you may use generative models such as RNN to serve yourselves with several plausible sounding names. Some could be catchy/weird and some surprisingly the exact ones you need.

8. ***Dialog System for Chatbots and Automation of Customer Experience***: Chatbots and bots are some of the most universal uses of ML. However, most marketing bots you observe in the wild are totally scripted and they use minimal ML and natural language processing. When the dialog systems are more sophisticated, they are able to refer to the external knowledge bases. They can adapt to unusual queries and also escalate to the human bots if required. Many companies these days have adopted the chatbots to communicate with their customers. They stay with the customers' right from when they have just learned about a new product or a brand onto after they have made the buy and need customer support.

9. ***Voice Based Searching Using TTS and STT***: It is considered as a part of conversational AI domain. The voice only or voice-enabled platforms bring a new paradigm and customer engagement possibilities inside the software and hardware interfaces. Due to the rising use of voice-based digital assistants like Google Assistant and Amazon Echo, the touch-free search and shopping are getting enabled. So now the marketers need conversational AI strategies as it is the future of marketing.

10. ***Brand Object Recognition by using Computer Vision***: Computer vision is a rapidly developing area of machine learning that can be lent to a range of applications. Marketers can make use of the machine learning powered vision for recognizing the product and extract the insight from the images on the labels and videos. Solutions such as GumGum permit the marketers to know when their logos have appeared in generated content and quickly calculate the earnings from video analysis. The more technically savvy marketers can make use of APIs

such as Clarifai to build customized solutions for moderating content and also for recommendation and search engines which are based on visual similarities.

11. *Original Media with GANs (Generative Adversarial Networks)*: Nvidia caused a huge uproar in the business community and created a buzz because of its methodology of generating photorealistic images of duplicate celebrities. Although these photos look like images of real people they are not. They are completely generated by ML and AI. By using the GAN (Generative Adversarial Networks) the Nvidia system became progressively more capable of creating ultra-realistic but fake images.

GAN has two competing networks, one is a generator and the second is the discriminator, which spar and learn from one another. Thereby they steadily become better at creating and also detecting fake images. Some other companies use GAN for creating logos, making photorealistic images out of sketches and also for generating voices.

12. *Automation of Robotic Processes for Marketing Operations*: Digital marketing is full of automated solutions aimed at making work operations easier for hard-pressed workers. Automated processes exist for opening and analyzing email attachments, reading emails, data entry for template reports and engaging and tracking social media triggers to allow the marketers to stay ahead on the curve. For the ads on the internet, there is an AI platform called "Albert" who decreases the human need for large-scale purchase of media, hastening the speed of necessary analytical computations and optimizing the paid advertisement campaigns.

13. *Superior Reporting by Using Automated Data Visualization*: Images speak better than words. AI is quicker and more efficient at transferring data to visual insights than any human

experts. The human analysts normally use tools such as Tableau or Excel to create virtual representations manually. However, the automated analytical solutions intended for businesses like Qlik can centralize the data sources to generate meaningful reports and dashboards for the marketing teams. Several platforms these days use data analytics with sophisticated machine learning algorithms to vividly clarify market trends. The behavior pattern of customers and other data that is hidden otherwise from plain viewing. This data is not easily available for conversion into practical insights.

14. ***Sequential Marketing Decisions Using Reinforcement Learning***: Many of the difficult decisions we make are not singular predictions and they are a series of decisions taken over a long period of time. Balancing the short-term trade-offs to the long-term benefits is tough for even smartest humans. The reinforcement learning is used successfully in DeepMind's AlphaGo to beat human decision making in case of complex scenarios. Although the business scenarios are far more complex than games, the success in case of smaller domains suggests similar progress in the larger ones. The IBM researchers conducted a notable study to explore the possibility of the use of reinforcement learning to improve targeted marketing.

Chapter 4

Machine Learning for Finance

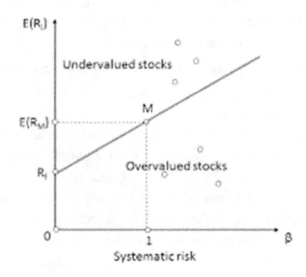

ML had useful applications in finance, even before the advancement of efficient chatbots, mobile banking apps, and search engines. Due to the high volumes, the requirement of the accuracy of historical records and the quantitative nature of the world of finance, very few other industries are more suited for artificial intelligence. You can find more cases of the use of machine learning in finance sector than ever before. It is a trend accentuated by greater computing power and more accessible ML tools such as Google's TensorFlow.

ML has arrived and plays a crucial role in modern society and in many areas of finance. It is involved in approving loans, managing assets and assessing risks. Although very few tech-savvy people have an accurate view of how many views are there in which ML finds its way in the financial lives of people.

Current Financial Applications

Here are some examples of ML being put to use in today's world. Keep in mind that some of the applications use multiple AI technologies or approaches and not just ML.

1. Portfolio Management:

Robo-Advisor is a term not heard of a few years ago but is now used commonly in the financial world. The term, however, is a little misleading as it doesn't involve any robots at all. Instead, the Robo-advisors (e.g. Betterment or Wealthfront) are algorithms based on ML and built to shape the financial portfolio of a user including their goals and risk tolerance. For example, users enter goals such as retiring at the age of 65 with $3,000,000 in saving. They also enter their age, current financial status, and income.

The advisor who can be more accurately referred to as an allocator then spends the investments across assets classes and financial instruments to arrive at the user's goals. The advisor system then calibrates to the changes in user's goals and to the actual changes in the market thereby finding the best fit for the user's goals. They have gained significant importance among consumers that do not need physical advisors to feel comfortable in investments and those who are incapable of paying fees to human advisors.

2. Trading with Algorithm:

Algorithm trading goes as far back as the 1970s and is also called automated trading systems. It makes use of difficult AI systems to agree on very fast trading decisions. The algorithmic systems make thousands or millions of trades in one day. Therefore the term HFT (High-Frequency Trading) is used and it is a part of algorithmic trading. Most of the financial institutions and hedge funds don't disclose their AI approach they are using for trading. However, it is believed that deep learning and ML are playing a rising important role in trading decisions. There are some exceptional limitations to the use of ML in trading stocks.

3. Detecting Fraud:

The system can detect abnormal behavior or unique activities by using machine learning and flag them to the security department. The main challenge for this system is to avoid false positives and situations where risks get flagged when actually there aren't any. There are a high number of ways in which security can get breached, so genuine learning systems will become a necessity in coming 5 to 10 years.

4. Insurance or Loan Underwriting:

Underwriting can be described as the perfect job for ML in finance, but there is a lot of worry in the market that the machines will replace many of underwriting positions in existence today. This is especially a concern in large organizations, such as large banks and public limited insurance companies. Machine learning algorithms can be trained on millions of instances of consumer data such as jobs, age, marital status etc. It can also be used for insurance results and financial lending in checking whether a person defaulted or not or is paying his loans on time or has been involved in a car accident.

The underlying trends can be assessed by using algorithms and analyzed constantly to detect trends that influence lending and insurance for the future. For example, you can find whether more and more youngsters are getting into car accidents. Or is there an increasing rate of defaults among a specific demography in the last 10 years? The results of these queries have a great yield for the organizations. However, this is limited at the moment to large companies having the resources to get data scientists and possessing the massive amount of data (past and present) to train the algorithms.

Machine Learning and Cryptocurrencies

The AI and machine learning assisted trading has attracted huge interest in the last few years. There is a hypothesis that the inefficiencies in the cryptocurrency markets can be used to create large profits. The normal trading strategies helped by the state of the art ML algorithms are far more capable than the standard benchmarks. Some nontrivial, but actually simple algorithms, can aid in anticipating the short-term evolution of cryptocurrencies market.

The success that ML techniques had with the predictions of stock markets suggested that the methods could be used effectively to predict the cryptocurrency prices as well. But applying the ML algorithm to the cryptocurrency market is limited mainly to analyzing the Bitcoin prices by using the Bayesian neural network, random forests, long and short-term memory neural networks and some other algorithms. These studies anticipated to a degree the price fluctuations of Bitcoin and concluded that the best results could be achieved by using algorithms that were based on neural networks. The reinforcement deep learning was able to beat the performance of buy and hold strategies in predicting the prices of 12 different cryptocurrencies over a period of one year. There were other attempts to use ML for predicting prices of cryptocurrencies other than Bitcoin however they came from non-academic resources and did not provide comparisons for the results.

Day Trading with Machine Learning

The speculation in securities is called day trading. More specifically it refers to buying and selling financial instruments on the same day of trading. Strictly speaking, it is a trading happening within a single day. It means that all positions get closed when the market is closed for the day. The day traders look at identifying the entry and exit positions on the stocks that have favorable conditions. These conditions yield several small term profits that can add up to big gains.

In case there are people in the market who can recognize favorable patterns in the market than we can train even a machine to perform similarly and even at superhuman levels. This is the goal of using machine learning for day trading. But first, we need to identify the strategies used by day traders to signal entry conditions in the market. The technique is split into two processes: a high-level pattern description and the second is machine learning.

In the first process, identifying entry semantics, which occurs for possibly hundreds of predefined strategies. This is done by using robust and highly scalable pattern matchers, such as Apache Flink. Once a pattern has been triggered we can go through the historical data and find the instances in the past when patterns were triggered and there was the outcome price after 10 or 20 minutes. We can generate a training example for the algorithms where we use machine learning for creating probability distribution about the past entries.

Conclusion

Because of the unique benefits of machine learning - especially on small devices - it is clearly becoming a favorite with businesses. From RPA functions to mobile automation it is all becoming a handheld reality bringing the future into the palm of your hands. Nowadays even smaller businesses can leverage ML like the bigger boys. It can be used in cost-effective ways. For example, some companies use AI for improving customer relations. It reduces the costs and at the same time provides customized assistance to their companies. It can also be utilized to train the workforce and to improve forecasting cost-effectively. For example, Udacity, which is an educational institution, enhanced their sales by 50% by introducing chatbots to their sales teams. The advancements in data, algorithms and infrastructure and the costs required for getting them has decreased their overall costing and nowadays smaller businesses can afford them.

However, there are a host of questions raised about ethics in relation to machine learning. Systems that are trained on data sets with biases might lead to digitalization of cultural prejudices. For example, using data from a job hiring firm with racist policies will lead to machine learning systems duplicating the bias during the selection of applicants. Collecting "responsible data" and proper documentation of rules for algorithms to be used by systems has become significant. Even the languages contain biases and ML will have to learn them. Healthcare professionals developing the machines for generating income rather than serving people is another concern. There are some shining advantages as well. As AI will increase productivity in many jobs, although lower and middle-level positions may be eliminated. However, several new positions with highly skilled, medium skilled and even low skilled range of people will be required.

Machine Learning is the way of the future and to the success of your business.

References

https://en.wikipedia.org/wiki/Machine_learning

https://news.sophos.com/en-us/2017/09/21/man-vs-machine-comparing-artificial-and-biological-neural-networks/

https://towardsdatascience.com/a-machine-learning-approach-building-a-hotel-recommendation-engine-6812bfd53f50

https://towardsdatascience.com/clustering-algorithms-for-customer-segmentation-af637c6830ac

https://www.distrelec.de/current/en/artificial-intelligence/will-machine-learning-surpass-human-learning/

https://www.ubs.com/microsites/artificial-intelligence/en/ai-coming-age.html

https://www.upwork.com/hiring/data/neural-networks-demystified/

MACHINE LEARNING

Master Machine Learning
for Aspiring Data Scientists

MG Martin

Introduction

Many people consider machine learning to be the road to riches, the road that leads to artificial intelligence. And it may well be, but for data scientists, for businessmen, and for statisticians, it the most powerful tool at their disposal, a tool that allows them to achieve predictive results of an unprecedented level.

Before we dive into the whys and wherefores of machine learning for data science, it is worth spending a bit of time talking about why it is so important. Most people already know something about artificial intelligence and normally when we hear about it, we think of robots doing the same things that humans do. It is important to understand that, while there are easy tasks, there are also difficult ones and a time when robots take over most human tasks is a long way off.

However, machine learning is here, and it is here to stay. Artificial intelligence is a branch of machine learning and just about every AI task is based on machine learning. Not so long ago, there was a common belief that robots would need to learn everything they know from humans. The human brain is a highly sophisticated organ and it isn't easy to describe every action it co-ordinates. In 1959 Arthur Samuel came up with the idea that, rather than teaching computers, we could make them learn instead. He was also responsible for the term 'machine learning' and now, whenever we talk of machine learning, we are referring to computers learning tasks autonomously.

Some examples of machine learning that some people may not realize are machine learning include:

1. **Natural Language Processing** – otherwise called NLP. A good example of this is translation apps, such as Google Translate. This isn't backed by a standard dictionary, it is a set

of algorithms that updates itself based on the way different words are used.

2. **Voice Assistants** – such as Alexa, Siri, Google Assistant, and Cortana. These are all examples of technologies based on speech recognition and all of them are built on machine learning algorithms.

3. **Spam Filters** – every email provider has a spam filter, keeping unwanted email out of your inbox. Machine learning algorithms are used to learn what is and isn't spam, learning better as they filter more emails.

4. **Recommendation Systems** – you see it on Amazon, Netflix, YouTube, even Facebook. All recommendations are made based on your search activity, behavior, likes, follows, and more. No human could ever produce recommendations as well-suited and, while there are those who believe it to be intrusive, this is the type of data that is far too complex for humans to process. Machines match sellers and buyers, books with readers, movies with viewers and more. And Amazon has taken things even further. The algorithms they use are so good, they can pretty much predict what you will buy and when and they are so confident of that, they will send the product to the warehouse nearest you, allowing you to get it same or next day as you order it.

Some machine learning instances that are already here revolve around the financial sector. Machine learning algorithms can do what humans can't – they can respond to changes in the market quicker than you can even think about it.

You can predict whether an employee is likely to leave for another job, whether a customer will buy or go to a competitor, or just not make any purchase at all. Sales can be predicted, hidden opportunities

110

uncovered, and so much more. Machine learning opens the door to a multitude of opportunities and there is no end in sight to what it can do.

And then we have the self-drive cars, something that we only saw in films until just recently. Now, millions of miles have been covered by these cars and it was all done using algorithms that allow the car to learn how to drive efficiently and safely.

I could go on and on but I won't. I'm sure you can see why machine learning is so important so, what I am going to discuss here is the process behind it. There will be a few code examples but not many – this is mostly theory but I have tried to keep it light-hearted. I covered much of the practical side in my other books so, for this book, you should have a good idea as to what to expect. If you read those guides, you will have the experience necessary to start this one so I suggest that you work through this guide using your own data.

Data Science is a tough field to get into and mastering machine learning is a vital part of that field.

Chapter 1

A Look at Machine Learning Algorithms

Before we can really get started on our journey, we need to clear up a huge misconception that surrounds machine learning – it is NOT about algorithms.

Open any syllabus or university textbook and you will be confronted with a long list of algorithms and that is one of the fuels igniting the misconception. Yes, you do need to learn lots of different algorithms but machine learning is about so much more.

It is one of the most comprehensive approaches to problem-solving and each algorithm is just one tiny part of that puzzle. For the most part, the puzzle is all about applying those algorithms in the right way to get the right result.

Why is Machine Learning So Special?

Break it down and machine learning is about nothing more than teaching a computer to identify and learn patterns from the data you give it. Often, that is for the purpose of making predictions or decisions. And for real machine learning, the computer has got to be able to learn patterns it hasn't been programmed explicitly to identify.

Let's take a famous example, a curious child.

A young boy is playing in his home; there is a candle burning in the table so he goes towards it.

1. He is curious, so he puts his hand over the flame

2. He yells in pain, pulling his hand back

3. He identifies that the bright red thing hurt him

A couple of days later, he is playing in the kitchen. The stovetop is on so he goes toward it again.

1. Curious once more, he thinks about putting his hand over it again

2. Then he notices that it is bright red

3. He hesitates and pulls back, remembering that bright red means pain and he doesn't put his hand over it.

This is a basic form of machine learning – the young boy learned patterns from the candle and his own actions. Because he remembered that the bright red candle flame hurt him, he avoided putting his hand over the stovetop, which was also glowing bright red. However, had he avoided the stovetop because he was told to by his parents, that would be classed as explicit programming and not machine learning.

Key Terminology

What I want to focus on for now is a practical achievement, rather than getting bogged down in technicalities. There is plenty of time for that later. As such, it is important that you understand the terminology. These are the terms you need to be aware of:

1. **Model** – a pattern set learned from specific data

2. **Algorithm** – a machine learning process used for training the model

3. **Training Data** – the dataset the algorithm learns from

4. **Test Data** – a subset of the dataset set aside to evaluate the performance of the model

5. **Features** – columns, or variables, within the dataset; these are used for training the model

6. **Target Variable** – a variable that you are attempting to predict

7. **Observations** – the data points, or rows, in the dataset

Let's take an example of a dataset containing information about 150 primary school students. You want to make predictions on their Height, based on Gender, Age, and Weight:

1. There are 150 observations in the dataset

2. There is one target variable, which is Height

3. There are three features, which are Age, Gender, Weight

Your dataset will be split into two subsets:

1. 120 observations used for training models on – this is known as the training set

2. 30 observations used for evaluating and choosing the best model – this is known as the test set.

We'll go into this in more detail in a later chapter.

Machine Learning Tasks

Academic machine learning begins with algorithms and it focuses on them. With applied machine learning, the important thing is choosing the right algorithm for the task at hand.

A) A task is a specified objective for the algorithm

B) You can swap algorithms in and out, so long as you have the right task

C) Always try several algorithms because, to start with, you will not know which is the right one for the task

Machine learning tasks are separated into a number of categories, with the two most common ones being supervised learning and unsupervised learning.

Supervised Learning

This includes tasks for what is known as labeled data. That means we have a target variable.

1. In practice, supervised learning is generally used as a more advanced method of predictive modeling.

2. Every observation has to be labeled with an answer that is 'correct'

3. Then, and only then, can you build your predictive model. The algorithm must be told what is right while it is being trained, hence the term, 'supervised'.

4. We use regression to model continuous target variables

5. We use classification to model categorical or class target variables

Unsupervised Learning

Unsupervised learning revolves around tasks that have unlabeled data, which means there is no target variable.

In practice, unsupervised learning is generally used as a kind of automated signal extraction or automated data analysis.

There is no predetermined 'correct' order

The algorithm learns patterns from the data directly, with no supervision

The most common of the unsupervised learning tasks is clustering, used for identifying groups in data.

The Three Main Elements of Really Good Machine Learning

To build effective machine learning models, and build them consistently, to give you good results, there are three main elements:

A top-class chef – human guidance

Although the idea is to teach a computer to learn by itself, human guidance is still a very big factor and, as you will come to see, humans are required to make many decisions, the first one is to decide how your project should be road mapped to guarantee success.

Fresh ingredients – relevant and clean data

This is all about the quality of data – regardless of which algorithm you use, always stick with the principle of Garbage In = Garbage Out. Most data scientists will spend more time cleaning their data, understanding it and engineering features than they do on the actual models.

Don't overcook things – don't over fit your data

Over fitting is an incredibly dangerous machine learning pitfall because models that are over fitted have memorized noise in your training set rather than learning what the underlying patterns are. For example, if a hedge fund has an over fit model it could cause losses totaling millions of dollars; for a hospital, it could cost many lives. Of course, most applications won't have such high stakes but it still remains that over fitting is a huge mistake.

We will go over all of this in the course of this book and, by the end, you will understand everything.

The Machine Learning Blueprint

All machine learning journeys follow are based on those three elements and they all follow five fundamental steps:

> **Exploratory Analysis -** getting to know the data – this should be a quick step, very efficient

> **Data Cleaning** – your data must then be cleaned – keep in mind that better data will always beat fancy algorithms

> **Feature Engineering** – next, you need to give your data helping hand in focusing on the important stuff and you do this by creating some new features

> **Algorithm Selection** – find and select the best algorithms for the task

> **Model Training** – lastly, you can train the model.

There are a few other steps that you might need to do as well:

> **Project Scoping -** you may need to roadmap your project and anticipate your data requirements

> **Data Wrangling** – your dataset might need to be restructured into a format that can be handled by the algorithms

> **Preprocessing** – sometimes, you can make your model perform much better if you transform the features first

Ensembling – and if you combine several models together, you can enhance performance even more.

We'll be focusing on the five main steps – these ones will slot in quite nicely when you understand the workflow.

Chapter 2

Exploratory Analysis

In the first chapter, we took a brief look at machine learning and the path, as a data scientist, you will take. As you saw, most data science revolves around five main steps and this is where we start looking at those steps.

The first is exploratory analysis and you should NOT get this mixed up with summary statistics or data visualization. Those two are nothing more than tools, a means to an end.

Exploratory analysis is all about getting the answers to questions. It is all about extracting sufficient insights out of the data to make sure you are on the correct path and in this chapter we are going to look at which insights you should be looking for.

Why You Need to Explore Your Dataset First

Explanatory analysis has one fundamental purpose – to get to know your data. Making it the first job you do will make the rest of your project run much smoother in these three ways:

> You get some valuable tips for cleaning your data and these can either make your model or break it.

> You get some ideas for engineering the features, and these can take your model from being good to being truly great.

You get a feel for your data and this helps you to communicate the results and deliver a much bigger impact with your model.

The one thing, the most important thing, about exploratory analysis is that it should be fast. It must be efficient and it must be decisive.

Never leave this step out but don't dwell on it for too long either. There are tons of possible charts, plots and tables but you really only need to use a small handful of them to get to know your data sufficiently well.

In this first real lesson, we'll look at the best visualizations for the data.

The Basics Come First

The first thing to do is get the answers to some basic questions regarding your dataset:

1. How many observations are in the dataset?

2. How many features does the dataset have?

3. What data types are the features? Categorical? Numerical?

4. Is there a target variable?

Example Observations

The next thing you will want to do is display some sample observations from your dataset. This gives you a feel for each feature's values and it is a good way of making sure it all makes sense. You are not doing any rigorous analysis here, you are just looking for the answers to questions like these:

1. Do the columns look right? Make sense?

2. What about the values in those columns? Do they make sense?

3. Are the values scaled correctly?

4. Do you think that missing data will cause a problem?

Plotting Numerical Distributions

Next, you should plot the numeric feature distributions and, more often than not, the best way to do that is to use a standard grid of histograms. Some of the things you want to look out for include:

A) Unexpected distributions

B) Potential outliers that make no sense

C) Features that really should be binary

D) Boundaries that make no sense

E) Potential errors in measurements

This is the point where, if you haven't been already, you should be noting down any potential fixes. If something doesn't look right, like a potential outlier in a feature, now is a good time to dig a little bit deeper.

However, we won't be making any fixes until we get to the data cleaning step just so that we can keep everything organized.

Plotting Categorical Distributions

You cannot visualize categorical features via a histogram but you can by using a bar plot. What you want to be looking out for here is any class that might have a sparse class – this is a class that only has a few observations.

As an aside, classes are just unique values for categorical features. As an example, let's say that you had a feature named exterior walls; things like Stucco, Siding, and Brick would all be classes for the feature.

Look on the bar chart for very short bars – these are the sparse classes and they can cause problems when it comes to building the model. In the best-case scenario, they won't have much influence over a model and, in the worst case, they can cause over fitting.

One recommendation I would make is that you consider reassigning or combining some of the classes but we'll leave this until we get to the chapter on feature engineering.

Plotting Segmentations

Segmentation is one of the most powerful ways of exploring the relationship between numeric and categorical features. A box plot lets you do this. For example, working with the real-estate dataset, you could draw several insights, including:

1. Media transaction price

2. Min and max transaction prices

3. Round-number min and max – could indicate truncation

That last point is an important one to remember when you look at generalization later on.

Studying the Correlations

Lastly, you should study the correlations. These allow you to see relationships between the numeric features and the other numeric features. Correlations are representative of the way that features move in unison and are values between -1 and 1. There isn't any need to remember any math for calculating them; you just need to know that:

A) A positive correlation is telling you that two features will increase together. For example, age and height in a child

B) A negative correlation is telling you that, as a feature increases, so another decreases. For example, how many hours are spent studying against how many parties are attended

C) A correlation that is close to -1 or 1 is indicating a stronger relationship

D) A correlation close to 0 is indicating a weaker relationship

E) A correlation at exactly 0 is indicating there is no relationship

You can use visualize this using a correlation heat map and, generally you should be looking for:

A) The features that have a strong correlation to the target variable

B) Whether there are any unexpected or interesting strong correlations between any of the other features.

Once again, your goal is to gain insights, to get a feel for the data and this will assist you as you go through the rest of the machine learning data flow. By the time you have finished doing the exploratory analysis, you will have gained a good idea about your dataset, a few ideas for data cleaning, and maybe some ideas for when it comes to engineering the features.

In the next chapter, I will walk you through data cleaning.

Chapter 3

Data Cleaning

In the last chapter, we cast our eye over some data visualization techniques that help with exploratory analysis and we also looked at what insights you should be keeping your eye out for. Based on what you found using your own data, it's now time to get your data into shape and we do that by doing some data cleaning.

This varies with each different dataset so we can't possibly cover every single thing you may potentially come across. However, you can use this guide as a starting point, a framework that you can use every time. We look at some of the more common steps, like how to handle missing data, how to fix structural errors and how to filer observations.

Let's start cleaning the data.

Better Data Is Worth More than Fancy Algorithms

Data cleaning is one of those jobs that all data scientists do but none of them really talk about it. It isn't the nicest bit of machine learning and there are no hidden secrets or tricks to it. But it is the one step that can either make your project or break it completely and the professionals in the data science community tend to spend rather a long time on it.

Why?

Look at the title of this section – better data is worth more than fancy algorithms. That is one of the simplest machine learning truths and there is no getting away from it.

In simple terms, garbage in will definitely equal garbage out. If you forget everything else you ever learned, do not forget this point.

If your dataset is cleaned properly, even the simplest of algorithms can learn some impressive and useful insights from it. Obviously, the type of cleaning you do will depend on the dataset but you can use the approach in this section as your starting point every time.

Remove any Unwanted Observations

This is the first step in cleaning your data – getting rid of any observations you don't need in your dataset, and that includes those that have been duplicated, triplicated, or more.

Duplicate Observations – these tend to arise the most during the data collection phase usually when you:

- Combine two or more datasets from different places

- Scrape the data

- Get data from other departments or clients

Irrelevant Observations – these do not fit the problem you want to solve:

- If, for example, you wanted a model built around Single-Family homes, you would need observations for Duplexes or Apartments

- This would also be a good time to look back at the charts you produced during exploratory analysis; look for the categorical features and see if any classes stand out as irrelevant

- Doing all this before you get to feature engineering can save time and headaches.

Fixing the Structural Errors

The next step is to fix any structural errors, those that appear when you are transferring data, doing measurements, or any other type of housekeeping that could be considered as poor. For example, check for inconsistency in capitalization, or typographical errors.

This will mostly be an issue for categorical features and looking at your bar plots will give you a good idea of what needs to be done.

After you correct the errors, you will see that the class distribution is significantly cleaner. You should also check that your classes have not been mislabeled too, for example, two or more individual classes that should be the same:

- If, for example, you have Not Applicable and N/A are two classes, combine them into one

- Classes called information technology and IT should also be one class.

Filter the Unwanted Outliers

Outliers can be problematic with certain model types, i.e. regression models don't do as well with outliers as decision tree models do. Generally, if your reasons for removing an outlier are legitimate, the performance of your model will improve.

However you do need to keep in mind that an outlier is quite innocent until you have proven its guilt. Never, ever remove one for stupid reasons, like it's a big number – that number could be providing quite a lot of information to the model.

This really cannot be said enough – outliers should be left where they are unless you have a very good reason for getting rid of them, perhaps suspicious measurements that are most likely not real data.

Handling Missing Data

Missing data is quite tricky, deceptively so, when it comes to applied machine learning. The first thing I need to make clear to you is that, if there are values missing from the dataset, you cannot ignore them. They must be handled for one excellent reason – algorithms will not accept any missing values.

Unfortunately, the two ways that are recommended for missing data are actually not that good. Those methods are:

- Dropping the observations that have got missing values

- Imputing the values using other observations as the basis

The first option, dropping the values, is not good for the model; when you drop an observation, you are losing information. And in fact, it could be quite informative that the data was missing in the first place. Also, in real-world problems, you will most likely be making predictions on data even when there are missing values.

The second option, imputing the values, is also not good for the model because, when you fill in a missing value, you will always lose information, regardless of the sophistication of your imputation method. Again, the fact that there is a missing value is often quite telling and you should always inform the algorithm of missing values. Plus, even if your model is built with imputation in mind, you are not adding new information; all you do is reinforce the patterns that are already there from the other features.

The simple answer is that, because the missing value is information in itself, you should tell the algorithm that it is missing. The question is, how?

- **Missing Categorical Data**

If you have missing data in your categorical features, the easiest way is to give them a label of Missing. What you are doing is putting in a new class for the categorical feature, at the same time as informing the algorithm that there is a missing value and it gets around the issue that algorithms cannot have missing values.

- **Missing Numeric Data**

Where you have numeric data missing, the values should be flagged and filled. The observation should be flagged with a variable indicating that the value is missing and the original value filled with 0; again, this meets the requirements surrounding algorithms and values.

Using this technique allows the algorithm to estimate what the optima missingness constant should be rather than using the mean to fill it.

Once you have completed this step, your dataset will be robust enough that it can skirt around most of the common issues.

In the next chapter, we take a look at feature engineering.

Chapter 4

Feature Engineering

We've looked at reliable ways of cleaning datasets, handling missing data, fixing structural errors and filtering observations. Now we need to take a look at feature engineering, to see how we can give the algorithm some help and bring about improvements to performance. It is worth bearing in mind that this is the step data scientists tend to spend the most amount of time on.

What is Feature Engineering?

Feature engineering is all about taking your existing features and creating new ones from them. The data cleaning process is one of subtracting and then adding new features and it could be one of the most valuable things any data scientist will do to make their model perform better. There are three major reasons for this:

1. Key information can be isolated and highlighted and this can help algorithms to focus on the important stuff.

2. Data scientists can introduce domain expertise

3. Once you grasp the feature engineering 'vocabulary' you can bring in domain expertise from others.

What we will look at in this chapter is some of the heuristics you can use to create new ideas but, before we move on, you should know that this is only a small sample of what you can do – feature engineering is pretty much limitless in nature. However, the more experience you gain, the better you will get at this step.

Infusing Domain Knowledge

Very often, informative features can be engineered by making use of domain expertise, either yours or someone else's. Think of some of the information that you might want isolated – we'll use the real-estate dataset as an example here, using the housing crisis.

Let's say that you have a suspicion that house prices are going to be affected; an indicator variable could be created for any transaction during a set period. These are binary variables and they have one of two values – 0 or 1. They are used to indicate whether observations meet specific conditions and can also be used for isolating some key properties.

Domain expertise is quite broad and is definitely open-ended. At some point you will run out of ideas and that is where these next steps can help, a few very specific heuristics you can use for sparking ideas.

Creating Interaction Features

The first is to see if there are any interaction features that you can create. Interaction features combine two or more features. There are contexts where an interaction term has to be the product from two variables and, in the context we are using they may be sums, products, even differences between features. Generally, it is useful to look at pairs of features and see if you can combine the information in them in a useful way.

Using the real-estate example:

- Let's assume that we have a feature named num_schools – this indicates how many schools are in a 5-mile radius of a property

- We have a feature named median_school – this indicates the median quality score for the schools

- However, we may have suspicions that the most important factor is having many options for school but only good options.

- To capture an interaction like that we would engineer a new feature names school_score = num_schools x median_school.

Combining Sparse Classes

The next heuristic is to group sparse classes together. As far as categorical features go, a sparse class is one that doesn't have many observations and these can cause problems for some machine learning algorithms and lead to over fitting.

Things to remember include:

- There aren't any formal rules on the minimum number of observations per class

- It is dependent on the dataset size and how many other features you have

- A rule of thumb is to combine classes until each has got ~50 observations but this is just a guideline.

Back to our real-estate example.

To start with, similar classes can be grouped. If you download the dataset and look at it you will see that the feature called exterior_walls has a number of similar classes. You could consider grouping classes such as Wood, Wood Shingle and Wood Siding into one class you could label as Wood.

Then you can go through and group together all the other sparse classes into one class named "Other" - you can do this even if you already have a class called "Other." Some of the classes that could go into it at Stucco, Concrete Block, Other, Masonry, Asbestos Shingle, etc.

Once all the sparse classes are combined, you are left with a handful of unique classes, all of which have more observations.

Adding Dummy Variables

There are few algorithms that can handle categorical features directly so you these features need some dummy variables. A dummy variable is a set of binary variables, with 0 or 1 values, each representative of one class from a feature.

You are representing the exact same information but by using a numeric representation, you can pass the algorithm's technical requirements. After we group the sparse classes from the real-estate dataset, we are left with these classes, each translating to a dummy variable:

Original Class	Dummy Variable
Wood	exterior_walls_Wood
Brick	exterior_walls_Brick
Other	exterior_walls_Other
Siding (Alum/Vinyl)	exterior_walls_Siding (Alum/Vinyl)
Missing	exterior_walls_Missing
Metal	exterior_walls_Metal
Brick Veneer	exterior_walls_Brick Veneer
Combination	exterior_walls_Combination

Removing Unused Features

The last step is to get rid of any redundant or unused features. Unused features are the features where it doesn't make any sense to pass them to the algorithm, such as ID columns, some text descriptions or those that aren't there when the prediction is made. The redundant features are those that tend to be replaced by other features added during the engineering phase.

Once the data cleaning and engineering stages are complete, your dataset has been transformed int an ABT – analytical base table – and this is what your model will be built on.

Don't expect all your features to be great; some will make no difference to your model but that doesn't matter – one great predictive feature is worth 10 bad ones any day of the week. The key lies in choosing an algorithm that can choose the best features automatically from multiple options, thus avoiding over fitting.

In the next chapter, we look at selecting algorithms.

Chapter 5

Algorithm Selection

In this section of the guide, we are going to look at selecting the algorithms. Rather than discussing every one of them – there are a lot – we're just going to look at best practices.

There are two very powerful mechanisms in the modern machine learning algorithm – regularization and ensembles – and both fix flaws in older algorithms.

How to Choose an Algorithm

We're going to look at five algorithms, all different, for regression and at their classification counterparts too. Where applied machine learning is concerned, algorithms should be swapped with one another depending on what gives the best performance for the dataset and the problem. The focus here will be on practical benefit and intuition more than theory and math.

Why is Linear Regression Flawed?

Basic linear regression is one of the most common models yet it has some serious flaws. Simple linear regression fits straight lines and, in practice, they don't perform very well at all. In fact, you are best forgetting them for most problems. The biggest advantage is that they are easily understood and interpreted but our goal isn't to produce a research report after studying the data; it is to produce an accurate prediction model. For this, simple linear regression has two big flaws:

1. It is prone to over fitting when there are a lot of input features

2. It doesn't express non-linear relationships very easily

The first flaw is addressed easily.

Machine Learning Regularization

Regularization is considered to be advanced in many ways but it is quite easy to understand. So, the first flaw is the issue of over fitting when there are many features. An example will help us understand why this happens:

- Let's assume that our training dataset has 100 observations

- We also have 100 features

- If a linear regression model is fit with all the features, the training set can be memorized perfectly

- Every coefficient would memorize a single observation and there would be 100% accuracy on training data – it's a different matter for unseen data, though

- The model will not have learned the underlying patterns, learning only the noise from the training data.

Regularization is one of the techniques used to prevent the over fitting and it does this by artificially penalizing all the model coefficients.

- It dampens large coefficients, thus discouraging them

- It sets coefficients to 0, thus removing some features altogether

- The penalty 'strength' is tunable – more on this later.

Regularized Regression Algorithms

There are three types of these:

Lasso Regression

Least Absolute Shrinkage and Selection Operator – Lasso – penalizes the coefficient's absolute size. In practical terms this leads to coefficients with a value of exactly 0. As such, because some features can be removed completely, Lasso offers automatic feature selection. Don't forget that the penalty strength should be tuned and stronger penalties lead to more zero coefficients.

Ridge Regression

Ridge regression will penalize the coefficient's squared size and, in practical terms, this results in smaller coefficients, although they are not forced to 0. In simple terms, ridge regression will offer feature shrinkage. Again, you should tune the penalty strength and stronger penalties will lead to coefficients being pushed nearer to zero.

Elastic-Net

Elastic-net provides a compromise between the Ridge and the Lasso regression. This one will penalize a combination of squared and absolute coefficient sizes and the ratio between the penalty types needs to be tuned, as does the overall strength.

There isn't a best penalty type; it all comes down to the problem and the dataset. You should try out different algorithms using a range of strengths as part of your tuning process – see chapter 6.

Decision Tree Algorithms

So, we looked at three different algorithms, all protecting linear regression from the problem of over fitting but in case you forget, there is a second flaw that affects linear regression – the problem of not being able to express non-linear relationships very easily.

Addressing that requires that we move away from linear regression and that means a new algorithm category.

A decision tree will model the data as a kind of tree containing hierarchical branches. These branches continue to be made until they get to leaves, representing each prediction.

Because a decision has a branching structure they can be used for modeling the non-linear relationships. Staying with the real-estate example:

- Let's say that, as far as Single Family Homes are concerned, the larger the lot, the higher the price

- However, with Apartments, the smaller lots have higher prices

- This is a correlation reversal that linear models struggle to capture unless an interaction term is explicitly added and, for that, you need to anticipate it from the start

- Decision trees can capture the correlation reversal relationship easily.

However, the decision tree is not perfect and has one big flaw too. Allowing the "grow without limits" will result in them memorizing the training data and that, in turn, results in ever more branches.

In short, a decision tree without constraints is also prone to over fitting. So how do we use the flexibility that a decision tree provides without letting them over fit the training data?

Tree Ensembles

An ensemble is a machine learning method that allows predictions to be combined from several models. There are two very common ensembling methods:

- **Bagging** - this tries to reduce the chances of over fitting with complex models. It does this by training more strong learners in parallel with one another. Strong learners are unconstrained models; these are all combined together to smooth the predictions out.

- **Boosting** – this tries to improve the predictive flexibility in the simpler models. It does this by training a sequence of weak learners, which are constrained models (the maximum depth of each tree can be limited). Each of the learners will focus on learning from mistakes made by the one that came before it and boosting will them combine the weak learners to make one strong learner.

Both of these are ensemble methods and both approach the same problem but from opposite directions. Where bagging attempts to smooth the predictions using complex base models, boosting attempts to boost the aggregate complexity of simple base models.

Ensembling is a very general term but when a base model is a decision tree, it is called either a boosted tree or a random forest.

Random Forests

A random forest is when large numbers of decision trees (strong ones) are trained and their predictions combined using bagging. There are also two randomness sources for the random forest:

- Each tree in the forest can choose only from one random feature subset to split on – this leads to feature selection

- Each tree can only be trained on a random observation subset in a process called resampling.

In practical terms, random forests work well out of the box, beating models that can take weeks to develop. They get good results pretty much all of the time and there are few tough parameters for tuning.

Boosted Trees

Opposite to the random forest, the boosted tree trains sequence of weak decision trees, using bosting to combine the predictions.

- Each tree is allowed to go to a maximum depth and this must be tuned

- Each tree will attempt to correct prediction errors from the tree before it.

In practical terms, boosted trees have very high ceilings of performance and, following correct tuning, they tend to beat a lot of other models. They are, however, very complicated to tune, more so than the random forest.

What you should take away from all this is that the best algorithms will offer a mixture of automatic feature selection, regularization, non-linear relationship expression and/or ensembling. Those algorithms include:

- Ridge regression

- Lasso regression

- Elastic-Net

- Random forest

- Boosted tree

Chapter 6

Training the Model

W e have reached the final step, training the model. The hardest part is done with the cleaning and the feature engineering so training, or fitting, the model is relatively easy. We're going to discuss some techniques that have become best practice.

How to Train a Machine Learning Model

You might feel as though it took time to get to this stage but a good data scientist will spend most of their time on the every step that leads to this one. What this chapter will cover is setting up the process to ensure maximum performance for your model while preventing over fitting.

Split the Dataset

We'll begin with a very important step that often gets overlooked – spending the data. Your data should be thought of as being a resource in limited supply. Some can be spent on training the model, which means giving it to your algorithm, and some can be spent on evaluating or testing the model. What you can't do is use the same data for the two sets.

If you were to train your model and then use the same data for testing it, your model would most likely be incredibly over fitted and you wouldn't see it. Models have to be judged on their capabilities of predicting new data, unseen data. That means you need to split your dataset into two – a training set and a test set.

The training set is used for fitting and tuning the model whereas the test set is unseen data, new data that your model will be tested on. So, the very first thing you need to do is split the dataset otherwise you will not get very reliable estimates of the way your model performs. Once you have split the dataset, you must not touch the test data until you have chosen the model you are going to use.

When we compare training data and test data, we can avoid the issue of over fitting – if your model shows good performance on the training data but not so good on the test data, you will know it is over fitting.

What Is a Hyperparameter?

In the last chapter, we mention tuning your model so let's look into it a little more. When we talk about tuning models we are actually talking about tuning the hyperparameters. Algorithms have two parameter types – the model parameter and the hyperparameter. The main distinction between them is that hyperparameters cannot be directly learned from training data whereas model parameters can.

- **Model Parameters**

A model parameter is a learned attribute used to define an individual model, for example:

- Regression coefficients

- Decision tree split locations

Model parameters can be directly learned from training data

- **Hyperparameters**

A hyperparameter will express the algorithm's high-level structural settings, for example:

- The penalty strength for regularized regression

- How many trees should be in a random forest

Hyperparameters are decided before the model is fit because they cannot be learned directly from the data.

What is Cross-Validation?

Cross-validation is a concept that will help you to tune your model. It is used for getting reliable estimates of how a model performs using just the training data.

There are a few ways that cross-validation can be done and the commonest one is called 10-fold cross-validation. This breaks the training data down into 10 equal-sized pieces, creating 10 smaller training and test data splits. The steps for this are:

1. Splitting the data into 10

2. Training the model on 9 sets

3. Evaluating it on the last set

4. Do steps two and three a total of 10 times, each time leaving a different set out

5. Average out the performance across all 10

That average is the performance estimate, or the cross-validated score and generally reliable.

Fitting and Tuning the Model

Now the dataset has been split into two sets, you know about hyperparameters an about cross-validation so now it's time to fit the model and tune it. All you need to do is the cross-validation loop in the steps above on every hyperparameter value set you want to try and the pseudo-code (high level) looks like this:

For each algorithm (i.e. regularized regression, random forest, etc.):

For each set of hyperparameter values to try:

Perform cross-validation using the training set.

Calculate the cross-validated score.

Once the process is finished, there will be a cross-validated score for each of the hyperparameter value sets for each individual algorithm.

The next step is to choose the best hyperparameter set in each of the algorithms so:

For each algorithm:

Retain the set of hyperparameter values that has the best cross-validated score.

Re-train the algorithm on the whole training set (without cross-validation).

Each of the algorithms will send representatives of their own to the end selection.

Choose the Winning Model

At this stage, you will have the best model for each of the algorithms tuned using cross-validation. The important thing is that, so far, only the training data has been used.

Now we evaluate all the models and chose the best one. The test set would be saved as an unseen dataset and that means it should now be reliable in providing estimates for the performance of each model.

There are a few metrics that you can choose and, while we aren't going to spend much time on them, the rule of thumb is:

- For regression, MSE (Mean Squared Error) or MAE (Mean Absolute Error) should be used, not forgetting that lower values are best

- For classification, AUROC (Area Under ROC Curve) should be used, not forgetting that higher values are best.

This is all quite straightforward:

1. For each model, use your test set to make predictions

2. Use the predictions to calculate the performance metrics, along with the 'ground truth' target variable in the test set

Lastly, you should ask these questions to help you choose the right model:

- **Performance** – which model showed the best performance using the test set

- **Robustness** – does it show good performance over several performance metrics?

- **Consistency** – did it have a good cross-validated score using the training set?

- **Win Condition** – does it solve your business problem?

Answer those questions and you have your model.

In the next chapter, we look at the five levels of machine learning iteration.

Chapter 7

The Five Levels of Machine Learning Iteration

I teration is nothing more than repeating one set of tasks to get a result but then you already knew that. Most books that you read, and indeed to a certain extent, this one, will focus almost entirely on the sequential approach to machine learning – load the data, preprocess, fit the model, make the predictions, and so on.

It is a reasonable approach, that is true, but in the real world, it is rare for machine learning to be that linear. In practice, it is cyclical in nature and that commands a need for iteration, tuning, improvement, repeating the cycle over and again.

Why So Much Fuss?

Iteration is one of the core machine learning concepts and it is important on more levels than one. The first step is to understand exactly where iteration comes into the workflow – if you do, you gain many benefits:

- You will have a better understanding of your algorithms

- You will find it easier to draw up realistic project timelines

- When it comes to improving your models you will find it easier to spot the low-hanging fruit

- If your first results are not good, it helps you to maintain motivation

- You can go on to much bigger ML problems

In fact, if you look at the workflow from the iteration perspective, it can help you to see the bigger picture so, let's not waste any more time; let's look at the five levels of iteration.

The Model Level

The first iteration level is the model level and it's all about fitting the parameters. All machine learning models, no matter what type they are, are defined by multiple parameters. Feature coefficients are used to define regression models, for example, whereas branch locations are used for decision trees and weights are used to define neural networks.

But that doesn't explain how machines learn the correct values for each parameter and this is where the iterative algorithm steps in.

Using Gradient Descent to Fit Parameters

Gradient descent algorithms are hugely successful, as is the stochastic counterpart. Gradient descent is an iteration method used for finding a function's minimum. That function, where machine learning is concerned, tends to the loss function, otherwise called the cost function. Loss is nothing more than a metric used for the quantification of incorrect predictions.

The algorithm will work out what the loss is for a model with specified parameters and will then change the parameters so the loss is reduced. This process is then repeated, or iterated, until the loss cannot be reduced by any substantial amount. That last set of parameters, the ones that minimized the loss, are the ones used for defining the fitted model.

146

Intuition

I won't go into the math here but you do need to understand the intuition behind gradient descent:

1. First, picture a range of mountains that have valleys and hills – this is the loss function

2. Next, every location on the mountain (the set of parameters) will have an altitude – the loss

3. Now picture a ball being dropped on the mountain – this is initialization

4. Any time now the ball will roll down the steepest slope – the gradient

5. It carries on rolling – iteration – until it can roll no further because it is in a valley – the local minimum

6. Your goal is to try to find the lowest valley possible – the global minimum

There are a few neat ways that you can stop the getting caught in the local minim, for example by initializing several balls, or providing more momentum so the ball can get over the smaller hills. And if you have a bowl-shaped mountain terrain, which is a convex function, the ball will always go to the lowest point – guaranteed.

In practice, it is unlikely that you will ever need to do a from-scratch implementation of gradient descent; you are more likely to use that already exist, such as Scikit-learn.

The Micro Level

The micro level is where the hyperparameters are tuned and is often known as the model family. Think of it as being much like a broader category, where the model structures can be customized. Some of the different model families include SVMs, decision trees, neural networks, and logistic regression and each has its own structural choices that have to be made before the model parameters can be fitted.

As an example of that, take the logistic regression family. Here, separate models can be built using L1 or L2 penalties (regularization). In the decision tree family, different models can each have different choices in terms of structure, like tree depth, criteria splitting, even the thresholds for pruning. Each of these is known as a hyperparameter.

Why Are They Special?

A hyperparameter is a high0level parameter. It cannot be directly learned from data using any type of optimization algorithm. A hyperparameter provides a description of the model's structural information and that has to be determined before the parameters can be fitted.

So, when you hear that a logistic regression model is going to be trained, for example, it is actually a two-step process:

- The first step is to determine the hyperparameters, e.g., should an L or an L2 penalty be used to stop over fitting?

- The second step is to fit the parameters to your data, e.g., which model coefficients can help keep loss to a minimum?

Earlier we mentioned gradient descent, helpful in step two but, for this to be used for fitting the parameters, the user first has to set the hyperparameters.

Using Cross-Validation

I am not going to spend much time on this section because we talked about cross-validation in the last chapter. It is an iterative method that you can use to evaluate models using specific hyperparameters and is a great way of reusing training data.

Cross-validation allows you to fit your models and evaluate them using just your training data and different hyperparameter sets. This means the test set can be saved as untouched for the final selection. Refer back to the last chapter for the steps on how to use cross-validation.

The Macro Level

The third level is all about solving the problem. Very often, you will not use the first model you create because it just doesn't work. And the same will be true even after you use cross-validation. The reason for this is because fitting and tuning the hyperparameters are just two steps of the workflow surrounding problem-solving. There are some other techniques that you could use and the next two are what we call low-hanging fruit and are used for performance improvement.

Different Model Families

In machine learning, you will sometimes hear about the No Free Lunch theorem. There are several different interpretations of it but we really only care about the interpretation that states, "There is no one model family that will work best for all problems".

There are lots of factors that get taken into account such as the problem domain, data type, data sparsity, amount of data, and so on, and they all have a different effect on how different families perform.

As such, perhaps one of the best ways of improving a solution is to try it on a few model families and the pseudocode for model family selection looks like this:

training_data, test_data = randomly_split(all_data)

list_of_families = logistic regression,

       decision tree,

       SVM,

       neural network, etc...

for model_family in list_of_families:

   best_model = tuned with cross-validation on training_data

evaluate best_model from each model_family on test_data

select final model

This is a type of nested iteration that is highly effective at problem-solving.

Ensembling Models

You can also try ensembling, i.e. putting several models together in an ensemble. One of the most common forms of this is to average the predictions from several models and, again, we talked of this in the last chapter. On occasion, you may see a minor increase in performance over one or more of the models and the following is the pseudocode needed to build the ensemble model:

training_data, test_data = randomly_split(all_data)

list_of_families = logistic regression,

decision tree,

SVM,

neural network, etc...

for model_family in list_of_families:

    best_model = tuned with cross-validation on training_data

average predictions by best_model from each model_family

... profit!

Did you spot that most of this is almost identical to the last technique? That makes things easy because you can double-up on both – first, use several model families to build a good model and then ensemble all the models. Last, evaluate each model individually and evaluate the ensemble using the same test dataset.

The Meta Level

This level is all about improvement. Remember at the start, we said that better data is always going to beat fancy algorithms but that doesn't mean that more data will do the same thing. Sometimes, better data does imply that there is more data but, more often than not, the implication is that the data is clean and relevant – better features can be engineered from it.

Data improvement is also iterative and the larger the problem you tackle in machine learning, the more you will realize that getting your data right from the beginning is nigh on impossible. You may have forgotten important features, or there isn't enough data. Whatever the issue, good data scientists always have their eyes and mind open to continuous improvement.

Better Data Collection

This is a skill that will accumulate over time and experience. Whatever model you are building, you need to collect in every single piece of information that is relevant to the model, no matter how small or insignificant you think it is.

The data has to be clean, which means the minimum amount of missing data, the measurement error must be as low as possible and you should, where you can use primary metrics instead of proxies.

The Human Level

This is the final and the most important of the five levels. If you forget all that you have read so far, never forget this section. The truth is this – data science and machine learning are huge topics and for beginners it can all be quite overwhelming. There is a lot to learn and, every day, there are new developments.

Even the most experienced find it confusing at times but the human level, you, are the most important part of it all. To finish this chapter, I want to leave you with a few suggestions, just to help put things a little in perspective and lessen the overwhelming feeling.

Always Learn

Iteration is an integral part of every single machine learning layer and that is the same as your own personal skills. It is a rich field and practice really does make perfect. The more you do, the easier it will be and the better you will get.

No Perfection to Start With

Nobody can build the perfect models right from the start and it doesn't matter if your first one is bad. Personal growth is the most important part, and your focus should always be on improvement.

You Don't Need To Know It All

Nobody does, especially where machine learning is concerned. The most important thing is that you lay the foundations that help you to learn new techniques and algorithms as and when you need to use them. And yes, iteration is a part of that.

Try Everything Twice

At least twice. No matter how hard you struggle with a task or with an algorithm, no matter that you are spending way longer than you hoped on something, always try at least once more. It will be faster and much easier and you will find it much easier to monitor your own progress.

Theory, Practice, Projects – Rinse and Repeat

One of the most effective methods of learning is to go through the theory, the practice and the projects and then do it all again, this time focusing on more targeted practice and much larger projects. This way, you get to grips with theory, you develop your practical skills and you are continuously improving.

Chapter 8

Strengths and Weaknesses of Machine Learning Algorithms

In our final chapter, we are going to take some time out to look at the strengths and weaknesses of some of the modern algorithms. What we intend to do is tell you what the advantages, disadvantages, and tradeoffs for each one.

One of the trickiest things to do is to categorize the ML algorithms and there are a few approaches that you can take. For example, you can group them into supervised/unsupervised, parametric/non-parametric, and so on. If you take a look on the documentation page in Scikit -learn you can see that they use the learning mechanism to group the algorithms, producing categories like:

- Generalized linear

- Support Vector machines

- Decision Trees

- Nearest neighbor

- Neural network

- And so on

This is not necessarily a practical way of grouping the algorithms because, where applied machine learning is concerned, you generally don't stop to think about whether you are training a specific model type. Normally, all you have is your goal and your algorithm is chosen based on this. As such, there is another method of categorization approach – going by the machine learning tasks.

No Free Lunch

We mentioned this earlier – the theorem that says there isn't one algorithm best for all problems and it really means something where supervised learning is concerned. For example, you could not state that a decision tree will always work better than a neural network, or vice versa, because there are so many different factors involved, not least the size of your dataset, and the way it is structured. In short, you need to try several algorithms for every problem, ensuring you keep back a test set of untouched data for evaluating the model; then you can choose the model that fits the task best.

Obviously, you shouldn't try just any algorithm, just those that are appropriate and that is where being able to choose the right ones is important. For example, if you were cleaning house you might use a mop, a broom, or a vacuum, but you are unlikely to use a leaf blower!

Machine Learning Tasks

We're going to look at the three most important machine learning tasks – regression, classification, and clustering. Before we begin though, there are two things of note:

- We are not going to look at any adaptations that are domain-specific, like NLP (natural language processing);

- We cannot look at all the algorithms because there are simply far too many of them.

Regression

Regression comes under supervised learning for the modeling and prediction of continuous numeric variables. For example, the prediction of movements in stock price, real estate prices, or scores on student tests.

A characterization of regression tasks is that the dataset is labeled and contains a numeric target variable. In simple terms, you have what is known as ground truth, a value for every observation that can be used for supervising the algorithm.

Regularized Linear Regression

Linear regression is the commonest of all regression task algorithms and, in its most basic form, it will try fitting a straight hyperplane – nothing more than a straight line between variables. It works very well when the relationship between the two variables is linear.

In practical terms, it tends to get left behind by the regularized versions, such as Ridge, Lasso and Elastic-net. The regularization technique is used to penalize the bigger coefficients to reduce the risk of over fitting – not forgetting, the penalty strength needs to be tuned.

Strengths – it is easy to understand and is easily regularized to reduce the risk of over fitting. Plus, you can use stochastic gradient descent to update linear models with additional data.

Weaknesses - it doesn't perform very well when the variable relationships are non-linear. They also do not have the flexibility needed to capture patterns that are more complex and it can be time-consuming and not easy to add the correct polynomials or interaction terms.

Regression Tree – Ensembles

Better known as decision trees, these tend to learn hierarchically by splitting the dataset repeatedly into individual branches, each maximizing the information gain for every split. This is known as a branching structure and is what lets regression trees learn the relationships that are non-linear.

Ensemble methods include GBM (Gradient Boosted Trees) and RF (Random Forests) and they take the predictions from multiple trees and combine them. While we will not delve into the mechanics of these, it is enough to say that the random forest tends to perform highly out of the box while the gradient boosted trees are more complex to tune but have much higher ceilings for performance.

Strengths – Decision trees can easily learn the non-linear variable relationships and tend to be more robust to any outliers. Ensembles are high performers and have won a lot of ML competitions over the years.

Weaknesses – individual trees that are not constrained are more prone to over fitting; they continue to branch until they get to a stage where the training data can be memorized. However, the use of ensembles can reduce this risk.

Deep Learning

Deep learning is all about neural networks with multiple layers. These are used for learning highly complex layers and make use of hidden layers in between the inputs and the outputs. This allows them to produce intermediary data representation, something that many other algorithms find it difficult to learn.

Neural networks have a few mechanisms that are important, including drop-out and convolutions, and it these that allows them to use high-dimensional data for more efficient learning. That said, a great deal more data is required by deep learning algorithms than by any other for training purposes because they have many more parameters that need to be estimated.

Strengths – it is the most up to date and state-of-the-art algorithm for some domains, including speech recognition and computer vision. DNNs (deep neural networks) show high performance on text, audio, and image data and can be updated with additional data easily using batch propagation. The number of layers, and their structure is adaptable to multiple problem types and the fact that they have hidden layers only serves to reduce the requirement for engineering new features.

Weaknesses – these do not tend to be very suitable for use as general-purpose algorithms, simply because of the amount of data they require. Generally, tree ensembles outperform them for classical problems and they are also very expensive in computational terms to train and tuning requires a lot more expertise and experience.

Classification

Classification algorithms also fall under the supervised learning umbrella for the modeling and prediction of categorical variables. This includes prediction turnover of employees, financial fraud, spam in email, and so on. As you will soon see, many of the regression algorithms will have a classification counterpart and these have been adapted for predicting class/class probabilities rather than real numbers.

Regularized Logistic Regression

This is the linear regression counterpart and it uses the logistic function to map predictions between 0 and 1. This means that each prediction may be interpreted as a class probability.

However, the models remain linear which means they work very when a class is linearly separable – this means that a single decision interface may be used to separate them.

Strengths – each output is probabilistically interpreted and you can also regularize logistic algorithms to reduce over fitting. Models are easily updatable with additional data and, like linear regression, this is done using stochastic gradient descent.

Weaknesses – it doesn't perform well when there are a lot of decision boundaries or they are non-linear and they are inflexible when it comes to complex relationships.

Classification Trees – Ensembles
The regression tree counterpart, both tend to be called decision trees or CART – classification and regression trees.

Strengths – they are good performers and robust as far as outliers go. They are also scalable and can model the non-linear boundaries easily because they are hierarchical in structure.

Weaknesses – individual trees with no constraints are more likely to over fit by ensemble methods can be used to reduce this.

Deep Learning
Deep learning can also be adapted quite easily to classification and this does tend to be the commonest use for deep learning tasks, for example, image tasks.

Strengths – high performer in terms of audio, image and text classification tasks

Weaknesses – like the regression algorithm, DNNs need huge amounts of training data and are not good for general purpose tasks.

Support Vector Machines

SVMs or support vector machines use kernels for calculating the distance between observations. Then the algorithm will locate the decision boundary that will maximize the distance between the nearest members of the individual (separate) classes.

For example, these are much like logistic regression algorithms and, in practice, an SVMs benefits usually come from modeling decision boundaries that are non-linear, using the non-linear kernels.

Strengths – these algorithms can easily model the non-linear boundaries and you can choose from multiple kernels. They tend to be more robust to over fitting, especially when used in high-dimensional space.

Weaknesses - they use an awful lot of memory, are much harder to tune because the right kernel must be picked and, where large datasets are concerned, they do not scale very well. Usually, the SVM is discarded in favor of random forests.

Naïve Bayes

This is one of the simpler algorithms and it is based on counting and conditional probability. In essence, models are probability tables that use your training data to get updated. For new observations to be predicted, all you would do is look in the table for the class probabilities, based on the feature values. The reason it is known as naïve is that conditional independence is its core assumption – that means the input features are not dependent on one each other – and this doesn't hold true in real-world problems.

Strengths – although its core assumption doesn't tend to hold true very often, these models do perform well, mainly because they are very simple. They can be implemented easily and are scalable with the dataset.

Weaknesses – because there are so simple, other models that have been fully trained and then tunes with the algorithms we already discussed tend to beat them.

Clustering

Clustering is unsupervised and is used for finding natural groups or clusters of observations based on the dataset structure. Examples of this are groupings of similar products, customer segmentation, analysis of social networks, etc.

Because it is unsupervised, which means there isn't a right answer, we tend to use data visualization techniques for evaluation. If there are pre-labeled customers, i.e. a right answer, in the training set, classification algorithms work much better.

K-Means

An algorithm for general use, K-Means used geometric distances in between two or more points to make clusters. These are grouped, surrounding a centroid, which results in them being similar in size and globular. This is ideal for beginners because of its simplicity and flexibility, provided data is preprocessed and useful features are engineered.

Strengths – it is the most popular of all clustering algorithms because of its speed, flexibility, and simplicity.

Weaknesses – the number of clusters must be specified by the user and this isn't always going to be very easy. Plus, if there are no globular underlying clusters, K-Means will only produce bad clusters.

That was a quick look at some of the more modern algorithms for classification, regression and clustering. Before you leave, I wanted to give you some advice:

Practice, Practice, and Then Practice Some More

While reading theory about algorithms can give you a good starting point, real mastery cannot come unless you practice. Find projects and work through them; this will help you to develop your own intuition and this will lead to you being able to choose any algorithm and apply it in the right way.

Master the Basics

There are so many different algorithms and we only touched on a couple of them. There are others that can be incredibly effective if used for the right task but most are an adapted version of what is in this chapter. These will give you a very strong basis from which to go on and explore more algorithms and, when you do, don't forget – practice, practice, practice.

Remember – Better Data is Far More Effective than A Fancy Algorithm

As far as applied machine learning goes, an algorithm is nothing more than a commodity, simply because they can be swapped in and out, depending on the task. However, if your exploratory analysis is effective, you clean your data properly and you engineer the right features, your results will be so much better.

Conclusion

First of all, I want to take the time to thank you for reading my guide. I hope, as someone who wants to be a data scientist, that you found this useful. Rather than giving you reams and reams of code to learn and understand, I have gone through the process of machine learning in a matter of fact way, although as lightly as possible. I have taken you through the fundamentals of machine learning, such as:

- What machine learning is

- The different types of machine learning algorithms, including regression and classification

- Data cleansing

- The downsides of some algorithms

- The ins and outs of machine learning iteration

- Training models

- Exploratory analysis

- And much more

Obviously, the subject is far more complex than this but I have attempted to give you a decent overview with enough information to give you a good grounding.

Machine learning is complex but it is also immensely satisfying, especially when you learn just what it can lead to.

I want to wish you luck in your journey to becoming a data scientist and hope that this guide has whetted your appetite.

References

https://www.analyticsvidhya.com

https://towardsdatascience.com

https://machinelearningmastery.com

https://elitedatascience.com

https://medium.com

www.ritchieng.com

https://www.geeksforgeeks.org

https://thenewstack.io

https://www.datacamp.com

https://hackernoon.com

https://dzone.com

https://www.kdnuggets.com

https://365datascience.com